Globalization
and the
Third World economy
Impacts and challenges
in the 21st century

Malthouse management series

Globalization
and the
Third World economy
Impacts and challenges
in the 21st century

edited by
Professor J. S. Odama
Dr E. A. Aiyedun

m a l t h o u s e ⋋𝒫

Malthouse Press Limited

Lagos, Benin, Ibadan, Jos, Oxford, Port-Harcourt, Zaria

Malthouse Press Limited
11B Goriola Street, Off Adeola Odeku
Victoria Island, Lagos
E-mail: malthouse_press@yahoo.com
malthouse_lagos@yahoo.co.uk
Tel: +234 (01) -773 53 44; 613 957; 0802 364 2402

Lagos Benin Ibadan Jos Oxford Port-Harcourt Zaria

© J. S. Odama & E. A. Aiyedun, 2004
First Published 2004
ISBN 978 023 184 6

Overseas Distributors:
African Books Collective
Email: abc@africanbookscollective.com
Website: http://www.africanbookscollective.com

Acknowledgements

We wish to express our sincere gratitude to colleagues from various universities and disciplines who responded promptly to our call to contribute chapters to this book. We understand and bear with some of our colleagues who due to unavoidable circumstances were unable to meet the deadline for the submission of manuscripts.

The authors were inspired by the urgent necessity of responding to the yearnings and curiosity of the general public, researchers and particularly our students, who challenged us to provide them with a comprehensive reading material on the phenomenon of globalization that has become a fundamental issue in world affairs since the later part of the twentieth century. This book represents our modest contribution to the debates and analysis of some of the critical issues arising from globalization, especially as they pertain to Nigeria and the rest of the Third World.

We are appreciative of the efforts of all those who contributed in one way or the other to the completion of this text. We remain grateful to our students who gingered us up to do this work. We thank all those who were involved in typing the manuscripts. Sule Magaji was in the forefront of the collation of the manuscripts and general coordination of the work. Mashi Abubakar did the initial typesetting of the work. Solomon Ogbu put finishing touches to the editorial work. We are grateful to them all.

Preface

The book is arranged into two sections. Section one addresses the general issues of globalization. This includes chapters by Professor Iyoha, Dr. Aiyedun and Dr. Ogbu. The rest of the chapters focus on globalization as it impacts on the Nigerian economy. In this preface we summarize the major issues raised by the authors in their chapters.

Professor Iyoha's chapter summarizes the developments in the world economy in the nineteenth and twentieth century. In particular the second half of the 19th century was one of rapid development among currently advance countries. Economic development in late nineteenth century was driven by the rapid expansion of world trade. The first half of the twentieth century was not one of rapid development. The two world wars resulted in the curtailment of global trade and international capital flows. The second half of the twentieth century proved to be a big improvement on the performance of the world economy before the Second World War. The basis of his analysis, Professor Iyoha provides some policy recommendation. These recommendations focus on the adoption of development strategies, which emphasize the following:

1. Outward-oriented trade policies;
2. Market-friendly economic and financial instruments
3 Promotion of private sector led development and market-friendly government intervention when deemed necessary;
4. Establishment of a conducive and friendly environment for foreign capital inflows;
5 Promotion of policies to increase autonomous productivity growth;
6. Adoption of economic and financial policies to increase mobilization of domestic savings and raise national savings rates;
7. Implementation of stable macroeconomic policies; and
8. Adaptation of measures to promote political stability.

Dr. Aiyedun's chapter is on nature and meaning of globalization: an African perspective. The chapter states that globalization entails universalization whereby the object, practices or even values transcend geopolitical boundaries. The chapter argues that it is from this vantage that we could speak of globalization of human rights, sustainable development, issues of environment, rule of law, democracy and good government. While the ability of developing countries in taking full advantage offered by the information technology -induced globalization is severely restricted by the stage of development of these countries, the chapter indicates that the development has transformed the scope, range, pace and the procedure of services delivery. Globalization has however encouraged de-intellectualization of the society, giving rise to the increasingly falling capacity to think for itself or to depend on externally generated and externally driven (concepts and paradigms) policies. This in turn has entrenched the dominance of expatriate personnel in policy-making and implementation in developing countries.

Dr. Ogbu's chapter is on the democracy movement and globalization; Nigeria in perspective. The chapter recommends that the political leaders in Nigeria must adopt a new psychological orientation towards politics by endeavoring to serve the nation to the best of their ability rather than pursue parochial interests and personal aggrandizement.

Dr. Alanana, in his chapter on the social and economic effects of globalization on Nigeria, examines globalization as a process of internationalization of capital and change, which is oriented towards incorporating even the most remote part of non-industrialized societies into the global capitalist system and market. The chapter cautions Nigerian government to slow down the pace of globalization to minimize its negative impact in the overall interest of the citizens, but should nevertheless embark on genuine programmes of self-reliant development.

Dr. Mohammed in his chapter on the socio-cultural impact of globalization in Nigeria traced the history of globalization to the imposition of imperialist rule by Western Europe and America, which nurtured a system of dependency and underdevelopment. Hence, since her attainment of political independence, Nigeria has been under economic subjugation. The consequences of globalization included the imposition of an unjust international division of labour with the country playing the role of producer of raw materials and provider of markets for manufactured goods of industrialized world. The value system in Nigeria, which emphasized brotherhood communalism and sharing, was substituted with individualism. As a consequence the social institutions such as those of marriage and family, education, etc, have been adversely affected by globalization. The chapter concludes by advocating a radical transformation of the Nigerian state and society through conscientisation and mobilization of the populace as a sure way of becoming an effective actor in the new globalization.

Dr. Aliyu's chapter explains the trade policy of Nigeria at different phases. The chapter also offers a model of international trade. The chapter concludes that Nigeria has many prospects to benefit from its involvement in foreign trade if it selectively embraces globalization process.

Dr. Ozigbo's chapter on effects of globalization on industrial productivity in Nigeria focuses particularly on the claim that increased economic integration has widened the productivity gains. The broad consensus of research is that globalization, both in terms of increased trade as well as increased capital mobility and foreign direct investment have only a modest effect on productivity gains. The chapter opines that changes in technological advancement have led to a pervasive shift in demand for foreign made goods, at the detriment of locally manufactured goods.

Mr. Magaji's chapter shows that Nigeria is embracing globalization with all optimism even when the country is not yet prepared for the new policy. The chapter suggests adoption of economic policies designed by the western nations with caution.

Mr. Nazifi's chapter hinted that the privatization of public enterprises as an aspect of neo liberal paradigm was implemented across the globe with Transnational Corporations playing a dominant role as core investors, providers of capital and technical advisers. The chapter concludes that economic empowerment of the populace must precede any divestiture programme contemplated if real transfer of economic assets from the state to the citizen is to be accomplished.

Mr. Obansa in his chapter on globalization and ecological problems in Nigeria, attempts to focus, in the face of globalized world, on the issue of good environmental management in an effort to address soil erosion, deforestation, water contamination, air pollution, and other forms of ecological problems on the Nigerian environment.

Dr. Mashi's chapter on Globalization and the Environment examines the real and potential impact of globalization on the environment. The chapter emphasized that environmental crises resulting from increased generation of wastes, environmental degradation, environment - induced social conflicts and aggressive exploitation of the environment would be encountered as we continue to promote globalization without concurrently promoting the need for better management of the environment.

Dr. Nwaobi's chapter on the 'new globalization era and digitalization debate: an economist's perspective' opined that during the post-World War II period, industrialization was an irresistible trend made global by the industrial society as it faces the risks created by its own success. Its growth has been accompanied by voracious use of natural resources and increasing inequalities (insecurities) between industrial countries and the rest of the world. Thus, a vision of a new society in which human lives in harmony with each other and with nature is very imperative. This transition is described as digitalization or knowledge revolution, driven by the technologies for processing and communicating it. This is therefore, an era where increasing proportion of economic output will be knowledge-intensive.

The book will be useful to students of the Nigerian economy. Policy makers and other stakeholders in the Nigerian economy should find and draw useful lessons in the various issues of globalization discussed.

Prof J. S. Odama
Dr E. A. Aiyedun
(Editors)

Contents

Contributors

Sani M. Abubakar,   PhD, Senior Lecturer, Department of Geography, University of Abuja, Abuja FCT

Ernest A. Aiyedun,   PhD, Senior Lecturer, Department of Economics, University of Abuja, Abuja FCT

Chika U. Aliyu,   PhD, Associate Professor, Department of Economics, Usumanu Danfodio University, Sokoto

Otaki O. Alanana,   PhD, Lecturer, Department of Sociology, University of Abuja, Abuja FCT

Nazifi A. Darma,   MSc, Lecturer, Department of Economics, University of Abuja, Abuja FCT

Milton A. Iyoha,   PhD, Professor, Department of Economics, University of Benin, Benin City Nigeria

Sule Magaji,   MSc, Lecturer, Department of Economics, University of Abuja, Abuja FCT

Suleiman B. Mohammed,   PhD, Lecturer, Department of Sociology, University of Abuja, Abuja FCT

Godwin C. Nwaobi,   PhD, Lecturer, Department of Economics, University of Abuja, Abuja FCT

S.A.J. Obansa,   MSc, Lecturer, Department of Economics, University of Abuja, Abuja FCT

Solomon O. Ogbu,   PhD, Senior Lecturer, Department of Political Science and International Relations, University of Abuja, Abuja FCT

Nathaniel C. Ozigbo,   Department of Business Administration, University of Abuja, Abuja FCT

Section I

General issues

Globalization and the patterns of development in the 20th century

– Milton A. Iyoha

Introduction

Economic development is deemed to have taken place if there is a sustained increase over a long period of time in the per capita output or product of a country. In recent times, it has become standard to define economic development as economic growth accompanied by structural change in the economy. This is not compulsory as sustained growth over a long period of years will necessarily bring with it changes in the structure of the economy. According to Kuznets (1959, p.14):

> Given the structure of human wants, a cumulatively large rise in a country's per capita product necessarily means a shift in relative proportions of various goods demanded and used - and hence major changes in combinations of productive factors, in patterns of life and in international relations.

This chapter will be mainly concerned with identifying the patterns of development among the developing countries of Africa, Asia, and Latin America in the twentieth century and isolating the role played by globalization. It is widely known that globalization, which is conterminous with increased economic interdependence and integration of the economies of the world, proceeded at an accelerated pace at the end of the twentieth century. What is less widely understood is that the globalization process was extremely active throughout the century. The forces pushing the globalization process have been many, versatile and strong. Technological advances in transport, the proliferation of mass media, and extraordinary innovations and developments in telecommunications have played an important role. Other factors that have driven the globalization process include the spectacular spread of trans-national corporations. But trade itself has played the most critical role of all.

In this chapter, the main focus will be on identifying factors and conditions that have promoted or retarded development. Note that even though initial conditions are important in the process of economic development, the rates of growth of output and per capita output are even more crucial. A good example is Argentina whose level of Real Gross Domestic Product (GDP) per capita was quite high in 1870 (see Table 1). Note that Argentina was more prosperous than Germany and Italy in 1870, and not far behind the USA In addition, its natural resources were vast compared to its population. However, it is now relatively poor because of its retarded growth, leading Madison (1970, p. 17) to describe it as "a drop-out from the developed world.[1] Note also that because of differential growth rates in GDP per capita, international income inequality has in many cases been worsened. A case in point is India. In 1870, India's per capita income was one-fifth that of the USA and about one-half of Japan's. However, in 1965, India's real per capita income was only one-seventeenth that of the USA and one-eight that of Japan.

Africa, the last continent to be colonized, has always been relatively poor. In 1913, Ghana's real income per capita of US$117 was lower than that of India, Mexico, Colombia, and Taiwan. Slow growth of African economies caused by a myriad of problems – the colonial heritage, imperialism, ethnicity, civil wars, and poor macroeconomic policies and recently, external debt has kept Africa at the bottom of the totem pole. On their part, Latin American countries have been backsliding. Though richer than Japan in 1870, Argentina is much poorer today. Latin American countries benefited from international trade but were apparently slow to modernize and industrialize. The domination of their societies by semi-feudal oligarchies and foreign commercial interests only served to slow down modernization and growth. Finally, poor macroeconomic policies, leading to hyperinflation and high external debt, have continued to weigh them down. Asia has had many success stories. This started with Japan. The Meiji restoration in 1867 signaled the rise of modern Japan. A well-educated class of Samurai, who were ready to make basic institutional changes and provide bureaucratic expertise and business leadership took over power and instituted a new tax structure, banking system and legal framework that were highly conducive to growth. The Samurai not only promoted local banking, shipping, insurance, export credit, and technical education but also created government enterprise in areas where the initial risks were large. In addition, they undertook agricultural research and carried out fundamental land reform. This led to the take off of Japan and its sustained economic growth. In the second half of the twentieth century, East Asian countries again came into the limelight with the phenomenal economic development of the Asian Tigers – Hong Kong, Singapore, South Korea, and Taiwan. These newly industrializing countries, whose development was driven by rapid growth of industrial exports,

---

[1] For more on this, see Kenwood and Lougheed (1970, pp. 21–25).

have now joined the ranks of the high-income countries. Not far behind are the ASEAN-4 (the resource-rich members of the Association of Southeast Asian Nations) - Indonesia, Malaysia, the Philippines and Thailand. They are following the examples of Japan and the Asian Tigers by demonstrating the benefits of outward-looking development policies. Then, there is the giant that has finally woken up from slumber – China. Emerging from isolation and promoting market-based economic reforms, China has surprised everyone by reporting phenomenal growth rates of exports (as high as 14% per annum) and GDP (as high as 9% -10% per annum) for two decades. It is now expected that China will join the ranks of the high-income countries early in the new millennium.

The history of economic development in the twentieth century divides itself neatly into two parts. During the first half of the century, i.e. until the end of the Second World War in 1945, economic development in many countries (both developed and developing) was slow, erratic, and unimpressive. The Great Depression came to worsen matters. Growth in world trade was also quite moderate. However, the situation changed in the second half of the century. Since the end of the Second World War, and especially since 1950, the growth of world trade has been rapid, technical change has been continuous, globalization has increased, capital flows have reached unprecedented levels, and economic development has been rapid in many countries. However, while most advanced countries and many Asian countries have reported rapid economic growth and development, many African and Latin American countries have continued to report low rates of growth of real income per capita. Thus, most African and Latin American countries remain in the ranks of the developing countries. An attempt will be made to analyse the reasons for the acceleration of economic development in the post-World War II period and for the differential performance between regions and between countries. This will permit us to demonstrate the important roles of international trade and economic policy in promoting development, and to extract important lessons. Using these, an attempt will be made to propose strategies for promoting economic development in Africa the years ahead.

In addition to this introductory section, the chapter contains four other sections. Section 2.0 analyses the global patterns of development in the years before the end of the Second World War while section 3.0 presents an analysis of the global patterns of development since 1950. In section 4.0 an attempt is made to elicit lessons from the global patterns of development in the twentieth century that may be used for policy advice in the years ahead. The last section presents a summary of the chapter, recommendations, and concluding remarks.

The global patterns of development, 1900-1950

A truly international economy fist evolved in the nineteenth century as a result of far-reaching economic, technical and other changes which triggered the massive expansion of capital movements, migration and foreign trade that took place during those years. The limited spread of industrialization before 1913 gave a powerful impetus to the growth of international trade in industrial goods in the nineteenth century. It also gave impetus to growth of trade in raw materials although this was moderated by the development of synthetic substitutes brought about by technical change in the chemical industries. Growth and trade was particular boosted by technical progress in transport and communications, and in industry and agriculture. After 1870, the focus of technical change shifted and this enhanced production and trade of steel, machine tools, electrical engineering products, and chemicals. Electricity emerged as a new form of energy and the internal combustion engine came to the forefront as the basis of a new form of transportation. The railway and steamship emerged, opening up continents and linking continents by trade. The result was a rapid expansion of trade in manufactures and an increase in economic development. However, the development mostly benefited the first world countries as most countries in Africa and Asia were still held in bondage by the forces of imperialism and colonialism.

Table 1: Level of real gross domestic product at factor cost per head of population
(Dollars at 1965 US relative prices)

Country	1965	1950	1938	1913	1870
Argentina	1,272	1,636	865	788	412
Brazil	482	351	231	-	-
Ceylon	271	241	208	-	-
Chile	863	678	595	545	-
Columbia	375	305	263	182	-
Egypt	295	191	178	176	-
Ghana	230	184	-	117	-
Greece	676	301	432	315	-
India	182	149	156	138	103
Israel	1,340	572	-	-	-
Malaya	528	490	-	221	-
Mexico	423	283	205	178	120
Pakistan	152	126	133	117	88
Peru	397	255	-	147	-
Philippines	269	207	218	201	-
South Korea	255	158	-	-	-
Spain	975	374	520	419	-
Taiwan	254	267	348	206	-
Thailand	289	159	-	-	-
Turkey	1,264	203	201	-	-
Venezuela	736	828	493	-	-

Country	1965	1950	1938	1913	1870
Yugoslavia	1,990	312	279	217	-
France	1,990	1,159	954	774	426
Germany	2,109	934	1,072	811	404
Italy	1,345	663	676	521	379
Japan	1,466	438	703	366	209
UK	1,985	1,394	1,236	1,037	658
USA	3,179	2,356	1,513	1,239	503
USSR	1,495	734	548	339	226

Source: Maddison (1970: 18)

Table 2 provides data on the growth rates of GDP per capita between 1870 and 1968. The differential growth rates in GDP per capita for the 1913-1950 and 1950-68 periods justify treating the pre-1950 and post 1950 periods separately. An examination of Table 3 shows that for the twenty-two developing countries in the sample, real GDP per capita grew at an average annual rate of 0.8% between 1913 and 1950 while it grew at the rate of 2.8% between 1950 and 1968. Thus the growth rate of per capita real GDP after 1950 was more than 3 times its rate of growth before 1950.

The slow and unimpressive rate of development in the first half of the 20th century is attributable to many factors. They include (i) the interruption of free trade (which held sway in the late nineteenth century) by the First World War; (ii) the interruption of massive international capital movements by the First World War; (iii) continued population growth (iv) reduction in the tempo of trade during the World Wars and in the inter-war period; and (v) the burden of imperialism and colonialism on African and Asian countries.

According to Maddison, the economic development of the poor countries was especially slow in the first half of the twentieth century due to (a) the fact that their development started when several of the developed countries already had a century of economic growth, (b) the fact that growth, once started, resulted mainly from the productivity gains of international specialization and not from high investment, technological progress and industrialization (as was the case for the developed countries) and (c) colonialism, political domination by developed countries, and subjection to various forms of foreign exploitation.[2]

In particular, note that colonial regimes inhibited the development of human resources, blocked access to managerial skills, and imposed commercial policy that allowed no scope for tariff protection as a way of developing domestic industry. Besides, the foreign companies based in metropolitan countries creamed off a monopolistic surplus and undertook little investment. Thus,

---

[2] For more on this, see Maddison (1970, pp. 22-24).

investment rates in colonial countries were low and insufficient to support autonomous growth.

There was no discernible regional superiority in economic development of developing countries before 1950. While per capita incomes were still higher in Latin America as a result of initial conditions, growth rates were generally low and displayed no systematic pattern. Some countries in Latin America, particularly Brazil, had respectable growth rates of real income per capita. But, then, others like Argentina and Chile had low rates of growth. In Asia, the picture was also mixed.

Table 2: Growth of gross domestic product *per* head of population 1870–1967 (annual average compound rates)

Country	1870–1913	1913–1950	1950–1967
Argentina	1.5	0.7	1.1
Brazil	-	2.4	2.1
Ceylon	-	-	-
Chile	-	0.6	1.6
Columbia	-	1.4	1.3
Egypt	-	0.2	2.7
Ghana	-	1.2	1.3
Greece	-	-0.1	5.5
India	0.7	0.2	1.6
Israel	-	-	5.0
Malaya	-	2.2	0.8
Mexico	1.2	1.2	2.8
Pakistan	0.7	0.2	1.5
Peru	-	1.5	2.9
Philippines	-	0.1	1.8
South Korea	-	-	3.8
Spain	-	-0.3	6.4
Taiwan	-	0.7	5.3
Thailand	-	-	3.2
Turkey	201	-	2.8
Venezuela	-	-	2.5
Yugoslavia	-	0.9	5.6
Average	1.0	0.8	2.8

Malaya had a respectable growth rate of income per capital but those of India, Pakistan and Philippines were atrociously low. On the African continent, Ghana managed to report a per capita growth rate of 1.2%.

The global patterns of development, 1950-2000

The rate of growth of global GDP began to accelerate in 1950 and the high growth rates have been essentially maintained to the end of the century. Most developed countries and many developing countries, particularly in Asia, shared in this rapid and sustained rise in real GDP. The growth of world income was pushed by many factors, including the rapid expansion of world trade, rapid and continuous technological advances and breakthroughs in transportation and telecommunications, massive flows of capital (both private and official), continued development of human capital and more efficient exploitation of natural resources. Tables 3, 4, and 6 present data on the growth rates of GDP per capita for selected countries in Asia and Africa and some developed countries. An examination of the data shows that while GDP increased on the aggregate, the most noticeable increases occurred in Asia. Indeed, if attention is focused on the rates of growth of real GDP per capita, it is clear that the most successful countries were in Asia, particularly in East Asia. By comparison, data reported by Naya *et al.* (1989) show that Latin American performance was pedestrian while the performance of African countries, with the exception of a few small countries like Mauritius and Botswana, was quite unimpressive, perhaps even atrocious.

First, consider Table 3 that presents data, *inter alia,* on real GDP per capita growth between 1960 and 1987. The rates of growth of real GDP per capita of the Asian Tigers during these three decades were nothing short of phenomenal. The rates of growth vary from a "low" of 6.1% for Hong Kong to a high of 7.4% for Taiwan. The ASEAN-4 also performed well, with the possible exception of the Philippines, which recorded an average per capita GDP growth of 1.70/0. The other three countries posted growth rats in excess of 3.20/0. China recorded a growth rate of 4.5% for the entire period but an impressive rate of 9.2% for the 1980-87 period. During the 1960-87 period, the average annual growth rate of per capita real GDP for the USA was 2% (Naya *et al.*: 1989, pp. 40-41) give comparative GDP per capita growth rates for Asia and Latin America and the Caribbean. Between 1950 and 1965, the average annual growth rate of per capita GDP in Asia was 2.8% while that of Latin America and the Caribbean was 1.911/0. During the 1965-1981 period, the growth rate was 5.6% for Asia and 2.911/0 for Latin America and the Caribbean. For the 1981–1985 period, the growth rate was 2.76/0 for Asia and -0.8% for Latin America and the Caribbean. Table 6, which presents data on growth of real GDP for African countries, permits a comparison with Asia, and Latin America. For all Africa, the average growth rate of real GDP between 1975 and 1984 was 3.30/0 between 1985 and 1989, it was 2.1% and between 1990 and 1997, it was 2%.

Table 3: Average annual rates of growth of real GDP and real GDP per capita

Group/Country	1960–69[a]	1970–79[b]	1980–87[c]	1988[d]	Per capita 1960–87[e]
NIEs					
Hong Kong	10.0	9.4	8.1	7.5	6.1
Korea	8.5	9.8	7.2	11.0	6.5
Singapore	8.9	9.6	6.4	10.1	6.5
Taiwan	11.6	10.1	7.4	7.0	7.4
ASEAN-4					
Indonesia	3.5	7.7	5.1	4.0	3.2
Malaysia	6.5	8.1	5.0	7.4	3.7
Philippines	4.9	6.3	1.0	6.4	1.4
Thailand	8.3	7.0	5.1	9.1	4.1
South Asia					
Bangladesh	NA	6.7	3.7	2.6	2.6
Burma	3.5	3.6	5.4	NA	1.8
India	3.7	3.2	5.5	8.1	1.7
Nepal	1.5	2.5	3.0	7.0	−0.1
Pakistan	5.0	3.7	7.1	6.1	5.4
Sri Lanka	4.8	5.7	5.0	3.6	3.2
Other Asia					
China	2.9	7.5	9.2	8.5	4.5
Developed					
Australia	5.1	3.3	3.4	3.0	2.2
Canada	5.7	4.7	2.9	NA	3.1
Japan	12.1	5.2	3.9	5.8	6.3
New Zealand	4.1	2.2	2.2	NA	1.6
United States	4.1	2.8	2.3	3.8	2.0

Notes: NA = Not Available; a = 1961–1969 for Singapore, Indonesia; 1962–69 for Canada; b = 1971–79 for Malaysia; 1974–79 for Bangladesh; c = 1980–85 for New Zealand; 1980-86 for Indonesia, Burma, India and Sri Lanka; d = Preliminary Estimates; e = 1960-85 for New Zealand; 1960-86 for Burma and Sri Lanka; 1961-86 for Indonesia and India; 1967-87 for Singapore; 1962-87 for Hong Kong; 1971-87 for Malaysia; 1974-87 for Bangladesh.
Source: Naya (1990; 4)

Table 4: Annual percentage change in world output by regions, 1970-1989

	Average 1970–79	80	81	82	83	84	85	86	87	88	89
World	4.5	2.2	1.7	0.5	2.7	4.5	3.4	3.2	3.2	3.8	3.1
Industriaslised Countries	3.3	1.4	1.5	-0.3	2.8	5.0	3.3	2.7	3.3	3.9	2.8
United State	2.8	-0.2	1.9	-2.5	3.6	6.8	3.4	2.8	.3.4	4.0	2.8
Other Industrialised Countries	3.7	2.3	3.1	1.0	2.3	3.7	3.3	2.5	3.3	3.9	2.9
Japan	5.2	4.3	3.7	3.1	3.3	5.0	4.8	2.5	4.2	5.8	4.2
West Germany	3.1	1.5	NA	1.0	1.9	3.3	1.9	2.3	1.8	2.9	1.9
Developing Countries	5.7	3.4	1.8	1.7	1.9	4.0	3.5	4.2	3.4	3.6	4.0
Median Growth Rates	5.1	3.7	3.0	1.7	1.5	2.9	3.1	3.4	2.7	3.0	3.5
By region											
Africa	4.4	3.6	2.0	1.2	-1.3	0.8	3.7	2.1	2.3	2.6	2.8
Asia	5.4	5.5	5.8	5.2	7.6	7.8	6.3	6.4	6.8	7.3	6.3
Europe	5.6	0.1	N.A	1.1	1.9	4.3	2.4	4.1	2.5	2.6	2.8
Middle East	7.3	-2.5	-2.1	0.2	0.9	-0.2	-1.1	2.2	-0.5	0.9	1.8
Western Hemisphere	5.7	6.0	0.2	-1.1	-2.4	3.5	3.5	3.9	2.5	1.4	3.4
By analytical criteria											
Fuel exporters	7.1	0.9	0.9	0.1	-0.1	0.6	1.2	1.0	0.6	1.2	2.3
Non fuel exporters	5.1	4.3	2.2	2.4	3.3	5.7	4.7	5.7	4.6	4.5	4.6
Market borrowers	6.1	5.0	1.9	0.4	-0.4	3.5	3.2	4.2	3.6	2.8	3.9
Official borrowers	3.5	2.9	3.1	2.4	1.8	2.5	3.0	4.0	3.3	5.2	4.2

Note: N.A.. = Not Available; Source: International Monetary Fund (1988)

Table 5: Net private capital flows to developing countries, 1990-1995

Country group or country	1990	1991	1992	1993	1994	1995
All Developing Countries	44.0	61.6	100.3	154.2	158.8	167.1
Sub-Saharan Africa	0.2	1.0	0.3	-0.8	4.7	5.0
East Asia and the Pacific	20.4	26.2	44.7	62.9	77.3	98.1
South Asia	2.4	2.1	2.8	4.6	7.4	6.0
Europe and Central Asia	8.2	7.1	21.6	25.0	15.6	17.3
Latin America and the Caribbean	12.2	22.7	30.4	58.8	49.7	33.9
Middle East and North Africa	0.5	2.4	0.4	3.8	4.1	6.8

Source: World Bank (1996; 11)

Noting that population growth in Africa lies anywhere between 2.5% and 30/0 it is clear that the growth rate of real per capita GDP was negative between 1985 and 1997 and barely positive between 1975 and 1984. Thus, of the 3 major regions, Asia performed best while Africa's performance was the worst. A further look at Table 10 shows that for sub-Saharan Africa, only 4 small countries – Botswana, Mauritius, Lesotho and Swaziland – performed consistently well during the 1975–1997 period. Kenya performed fairly well between 1975 and 1989 but could only report a 2.1 % GDP growth during the 1990 -1997 period. In North Africa, Egypt, Morocco and Tunisia came up with moderately respectable performances.

Table 6: Average annual growth of real gross domestic product in Africa, 1975-1997

	1975–1984	*1985–1989*	*1990–1997*
Sub Saharan Africa:	2.2	2.6	1.9
Excluding South Africa	2.0	3.1	2.2
Excluding South Africa and Nigeria	2.6	2.8	2.0
Angola	-	4.7	-1k
Benin	3.8	2.1	4.1
Botswana	11.4	10.3	4.7
Burkina Faso	3.6	4.4	3.2
Burundi	3.8	5.1	-2.8
Cameroon	8.5	-0.1	-0.9
Cape Verde	-	5.1	3.4
Central Africa Republic	0.4	0.7	0.7
Chad	-1.9	4.9	4.2
Comoros	-	1.3	-2.8
Congo, Democratic Republic of Congo	-0.3	1.7	-6.4
Republic of Cote d'Ivoire	9.2	-0.1	0.7
Djibouti	2.2	2.2	2.4
Equatorial Guinea	-	1.4	13.0
Eritrea	-	-	-
Ethiopia	-	4.1	3.5
Gabon	-0.2	-1.4	3.3
Gambia, the	4.3	3.3	2.4
Ghana	-1.1	5.2	4.4
Guinea	-	4.7	4.0
Guinea-Bissau	2.1	3.1	3.6
Kenya	4.7	5.9	2.1
Lesotho	4.5	7.8	7.0
Liberia	0.1	-1.2	-
Madagascar	-0.2	2.3	0.7
Malawi	3.3	1.9	3.5
Mali	2.3	3.9	3.0
Mauritania	1.6	3.3	3.7
Mauritius	3.6	7.7	5.2

	1975–1984	1985–1989	1990–1997
Mozambique	-	6.0	4.2
Namibia	-	2.2	3.5
Niger	2.0	4.2	1.1
Nigeria	-0.7	5.0	3.2
Rwanda	6.8	2.9	-5.5
Sao Tome and Principe	-	-	1.2
Senegal	2.1	3.5	2.4
Seychelles	-2.1	5.2	3.5
Sierra Leone	2.0	0.8	-3.3
Somalia	3.6	3.0	-
South Africa	2.6	1.6	1.2
Sudan	2.6	0.9	-
Swaziland	3.3	9.9	3.2
Tanzania	-	-	2.8
Togo	2.1	3.4	1.2
Uganda	-	3.4	7.2
Zambia	0.2	2.3	-0.4
Zimbabwe	3.0	4.2	2.1
North Africa	5.1	1.4	2.2
Algeria	5.5	0.8	0.4
Egypt, Arab Republic	8.3	4.1	3.9
Libya	1.6	-3.9	-
Morocco	4.7	4.8	2.2
Tunisia	5.3	2.4	5.0
All Africa	3.3	2.1	2.0

In Latin America and the Caribbean, the best performance was recorded by Brazil, which posted 3.6% average annual growth rate in per capita real GDP between 1970 and 1985. The island of Barbados was next with a per capita real GDP growth of 3.4% for the 1961- 1985 period. Six countries --Colombia, Dominican Republic, Ecuador, Mexico, Panama, and Paraguay --performed reasonably well, recording average annual GDP per capita growth rates between 2% and 2.7% during the 1960- 1986 period. Jamaica could only record a growth rate of 0.1% while Argentina posted a growth rate of only 0.2%.

Many attempts have been made to explain the high growth rates in per capita real GDP reported by East Asian, China and other Asian countries. The factors suggested have ranged from culture and religion to government intervention, and have included high savings and investment rates, massive capital inflows, economic reforms, education, and rapid export growth. In any case, there is little doubt that rapid growth in the East Asian, China and ASEAN-4 countries has been pushed by rapid export growth, large capital inflows, high savings investment rates, and good macroeconomic/commercial policies.

According to Kohli:

> The principal impetus to growth was provided by rapid growth in manufacturing, which in turn was greatly facilitated by a relatively favourable environment for exports, especially during the 1970s. Kohli (1989; 13).

Indeed, it is generally agreed that export-led industrial development has been the engine of growth in the newly industrializing countries (NICs)- Hong Kong, Singapore, Taiwan and South Korea. For example, the average annual growth rate of exports between 1970 and 1980 ranged from 23% in Hong Kong to 36% in South Korea (Kohli, 1989, p.16). This also comes into relief when compared with the performance of Latin America -while the share of exports in GDP in 1980 was 47.2% in Asia-Pacific; it was only 16.9% in Latin America. Similarly, the share of manufactures in total merchandise exports in 1980 was 47% in Asia- Pacific but only 22.2% in Latin America.

The investment rates in the Asia-Pacific region were very high both as a result of high domestic savings and large capital inflows. According to Naya *et al.*, in 1981, the average national savings ratio was 25.7% in Asia-Pacific while it was 19.5% in Latin America. From the data on net private capital flows to developing countries reported in Table 5, it is seen that East Asia and the Pacific obtained the lion's share of net private capital flows to developing countries during the 1990-95 period. For example, in 1995, East Asia and the Pacific got inflows ofUS$98. One billion out of total inflows amounting to US$167.1 i.e. 59% of total inflows. By contrast, sub-Saharan Africa got US$5 billion, or 3% of the total.

It is generally agreed that Asia has had more outward-looking trade and exchange rate policies than Latin America or Africa. Indeed, trade regimes in the NICs have generally been left to market forces. Where there were interventions, attempts were made to make them market friendly. A case in point is South Korea where protected industries were required to become competitive and begin exporting within a short period of time. This had the effect of promoting efficiency and competition rather than suppressing them

Other factors favourable to Asia as summarized by Naya *et al* (1989) are:

- Asia has had more market-oriented and less-regulated economic policies than Latin America. There have been more incentives encouraging entrepreneurship and private initiative in Asia; there also has been greater confidence in and between the government and the private sector - Naya *et al.*, 1989, p.6).
- Asia has been more concerned with macroeconomic stability than Latin America, especially with respect to inflation and debt management. Naya *et al.* (1989, p.8).

- Asia has had more political stability than Latin America (Naya *et al.;* 1989, p.11).

Technical change (or technological progress or total factor productivity) seems to have played a crucial role in the differential growth rates in real GDP and real GDP per capita in the different regions of the world. Invariably, most Asian-Pacific countries reported high growth rates of total factor productivity (TFP) while many African and Latin American countries recorded low, often negative, total factor productivity growth rates. This is perhaps not surprising as total factor productivity, also called Solow's residual, measures all sources of economic growth apart from those attributable to capital and labour. In a real sense, it measures the efficiency with which traditional factors of production are used and combined. It has been shown that if growth is largely driven by increases in total factor productivity, such growth could be sustained almost indefinitely, Iyoha (2000, p.3). Iyoha (2000) provides data on estimates of total factor productivity growth rates for selected countries in Africa, Asia, and Latin America. An examination of his data shows that the highest TFP growth rates were indeed reported by Asian-Pacific countries with Taiwan posting a 2.6% TFP growth rate. In Latin America, the highest TFP growth rate reported is by Chile (1.4%) while Peru had a negative TFP growth rate (-0.6%). In Africa, Botswana had the highest TFP growth rate of 1.70%. Nigeria reported a growth rate of 1.1% while South Africa could only record a TFP growth rate of 0.2%. Almost certainly, the determinants of total factor productivity growth are also the factors responsible for rapid economic development, as shown by studies of China, East Asia, and Nigeria. These factors include government policies (particular economic reforms), openness, natural resources, and initial levels of physical and human capital.[3]

Finally, during the last quarter of the twentieth century, the stubborn problem of debt overhang (high del-stock and unsustainable debt service burden) has emerged to further complicate Africa's development problem. There is convincing empirical evidence that the debt overhang has had the effect of reducing investment and lowering growth rates of GDP in many African countries (Iyoha, 1997 and 1999).

Lessons from the global patterns of development in the twentieth century

Alfred Marshall was right when he declared "the causes which determine the economic progress of nations belong to the study of international trade" (1959, p.255). However, he told the truth but not the whole truth. Trade is clearly

---

[3] See especially Maddison (1970), Elias (1992), Hu and Khan (1997), Sarel (1997), Iyoha (2000), and Young (1995).

favourable to growth and may well be a necessary condition for growth for small countries. However, it is not a sufficient condition for economic development. For sustained economic development to occur, the gains from trade must be complemented by autonomous productivity changes in the particular economy, savings and investment must rise, and economic policy must be favourable to private initiative, capital inflows, and the efficient use of resources.

The contribution of foreign trade to economic development is not in doubt. According to Haberler:

> Experience of the past thirty years or so has clearly shown that development policies that pay little attention to the vital contribution of foreign trade, private enterprise and direct foreign investment, do not yield sustained and efficient industrialization and growth (Haberler, (1988, p.5).

Basically, the "dynamic benefits" of foreign trade explain why trade is so crucial to economic development. Haberler (1988, p.27) provides a summary of these dynamic effects:

> First, trade provides material means (capital goods, machinery and raw and semi-finished materials) indispensable for economic development. Secondly, even more important, trade is the means and vehicle for the dissemination of technological knowledge, the transmission of ideas, for the importation of know-how, skills, managerial talents and entrepreneurship. Thirdly, trade is also the vehicle for the international movement of capital especially from the developed to the under developed countries. Fourthly, free international trade is the best antimonopoly policy and the best guarantee for the maintenance of a healthy degree of free competition.

In the general context of development policy, several authors including Krueger (1988) and Finch and Michalopoulos (1988) have established the superiority of outward-oriented economic policies over inward-oriented ones. Specifically, Finch and Michalopouls are able to establish that the economic and growth performance of countries with the outward-oriented international economic policies was on average, far superior to those with inward-looking, heavily protected trade regimes. Indeed, the superior performance of Asian-Pacific countries compared to Latin American countries during the second half of the 20th century provides sufficient evidence and validation for this assertion.[4] Part of the explanation for this result is that successful export performance requires economic policies that give adequate incentives for

---

[4] Several authors have also provided empirical evidence of the relationship between economic growth and export growth. See, in particular, Michaely (1977) and Iyoha (1998).

increased investment in the export sector. Nor is it purely a demand-driven phenomenon where increased export growth merely stimulates output. Rather, according to Finch and Michalopoulos (1988, p. 132):

> ...effective participation in international trade permits economies of scale not open to small protected economies. By introducing greater market competition, it encourages a more efficient utilization of resources and greater growth in productivity in the whole economy. Moreover, open trading policies permit quicker adaptation to new technologies and greater flexibility in responding to international economic developments.

To sum up, the main factors that explain the acceleration of economic development in the second half of the twentieth century and explain differential growth rates in per capita real GDP among developing countries include: (i) the extent of participation in international trade; (ii) international economic policy orientation; (iii) adoption of economic (market-friendly) reforms; (iv) favourable institutional and legal frameworks; (v) favourable external factors for foreign investment and official capital flows; (vi) favourable external factors (demand, favourable terms of trade, etc); (vii) adaptability to new ideas, processes, and technologies; (viii) stable macroeconomic policies; and (ix) political stability.

Capital flows, both official and private, played an important role in the development of the developing countries in the second half of the twentieth century. Table 8 provides data on net long- term resource flows (private and aggregate) to developing countries in the last decade of the twentieth century. The trend towards private flows is evident. By the end of the twentieth century, private capital flows had seized primacy from official flows as the leading source of development finance for developing countries. Countries with political stability, a conducive policy environment and high growth rates garnered the lion's share of net long-term capital flows as shown in Table 9. Inevitably the East Asia and Pacific region obtained a disproportionate share of capital flows to developing countries, which further served to increase their already burgeoning growth rates of real GDP per capita.

Lessons to be drawn from the global patterns of development in the 20th century flow from the analysis already presented and the factors already identified as critical to rapid and sustained economic development. These may be summarized as follows:

- adoption of outward-oriented international economic policies;
- adoption of economic reforms that are market-friendly and which encourage private initiative;
- adoption of economic, trade, and investment policies that encourage capital inflows and foreign direct investment;
- adoption of policies to encourage the mobilization of domestic savings and promote high national savings rate;

- implementation of stable macroeconomic policies;
- increased investment in infrastructure, education and health; and
- adoption of policies and measures to promote social cohesion and political stability.

It seems apparent that the most important single lesson from the success stories of the twentieth century is that policy matters. It is therefore incumbent on African countries to adopt policies and strategies in the economic, trade, and investment spheres that are conducive to rapid development. These, in general, will include outward-oriented, market-friendly and investment-friendly policies. Only in this way can they hope to accelerate their rates of development in the new millennium.

Summary and conclusion

In this chapter, an attempt has been made to analyze the role of globalization in the patterns of development in the twentieth century. After defining economic development as sustained growth in real per capita GDP over a long period of time, the chapter went on to undertake a panoramic review of global development patterns in the nineteenth and twentieth centuries. In particular, it was found that the second half of the nineteenth century was one of rapid development among currently advanced countries. Economic development in late 19th century was driven by the rapid expansion of world trade, buoyed by the policies of free trade and *laissez-faire*; massive international flows of capital; and rapid technological progress. The first half of the twentieth century was not one of rapid development. The two world wars did not help matters as they resulted in the curtailment of global trade and international capital flows. The Great Depression of the early 1930s only served to worsen the situation. The end of the Gold Standard and competitive depreciations in the 1930s further aggravated an already bad situation. The second half of the twentieth century proved to be a big improvement on the performance of the world economy before the Second World War. The establishment of the Bretton Woods institutions set the stage for an unprecedented growth of world trade which together with rapid technological advances in transportation and communication including the proliferation of mass media triggered an acceleration of world income and the economic development of many advanced and some developing countries.

The analysis showed that economic development was not evenly spread among developing countries or even among regions in the Third World. In particular, Asian countries, especially the NICs and the ASEAN-4 had very rapid growth rates of real per capita income. Most countries in Africa had low growth rates and sub-Saharan Africa as a region had a negative growth rate of per capita real GDP in the last quarter of the twentieth century. Latin America and the Caribbean did not do much better. A few countries like Brazil made progress but others like Argentina only retrogressed. The chapter then attempted to explain the differential performance in economic development of Asia on the one hand and Africa and Latin America on the other. It was found that the differential growth performance was largely attributable to policy performance. Asian countries in the main followed policies which emphasized trade openness, private sector initiative, high savings and investments rates, macroeconomic stability and political stability.

The analytical section of the chapter ended by attempting to draw salient lessons for policy advice from the success stories of the twentieth century .The policy advice to developing countries of Africa is to adopt development strategies which emphasize the following: (i) outward-oriented trade policies; (ii) market-friendly economic and financial policies; (iii) promotion of private-sector led development and market-friendly government intervention when deemed necessary; (iv) establishment of a conducive and friendly environment for foreign capital inflows; (v) promotion of policies to increase autonomous productivity growth; (vi) adoption of economic and financial policies to increase mobilization of domestic savings and raise national savings rates; (vii) implementation of stable macroeconomic policies; and (viii) adoption of measures to promote political stability.

Many African countries have the natural resources and human ingenuity that can support rapid economic development. It is believed that adoption and implementation of the proper economic and trade policies will enable many of them to improve their economic performance and record sustained economic development in the years ahead.

References

Akarnatsu, K. (1962) "A historical pattern of economic growth in developing countries," *The Developing Economics* (March -August).

Chenery, H. B. and M. Syrquin (1975) *Patterns of Development, 1950-1970*, London: Oxford University Press.

Chenery, R and L. Taylor (1968) "Development patterns among countries and over time," *Review of Economics and Statistics,* November.

Corden, W. M. (1974) *Trade Policy and Economic Welfare,* London: Oxford University Press.

Elias, V. J. (1992) *Sources of Growth: A Study of Seven Latin American Economies,* San Francisco: ICS Press.

Finch, D. and C. Michalopoulos (1988) 'Development, trade and international organizations," in A.O. Krueger (ed.), *Development with Trade: LDCs and the International Economy,* San Francisco, California: ICEG.

Harbeler, G. (1988) *International Trade and Economic Development,* San Francisco, California: ICEG.

Hu, Z. and M. Khan (1997) "Why is China growing so fast?" *IMF Staff Papers,* 44(1).

International Monetary Fund (1988) *World Economic Outlook,* October, Washington, DC.

Iyoha, M. A. (1995) "Traditional and contemporary theories of external trade," in A.H Ekpo (ed.), *External Trade And Economic Development in Nigeria.* Selected papers for the 1995 Annual Conference of the Nigerian Economic Society, lbadan: NES.

Iyoha, M. A. (1997) "An econometric study of debt overhang, debt reduction, investment and economic growth in Nigeria," *NCEMA Monograph No.8.* Ibadan: NCEMA.

Iyoha, M. A. (1998) "An econometric analysis of the impact of trade on economic growth in ECOWAS countries," *Nigerian Economic and Financial Review, Vol.* 3, December.

Iyoha, M. A. (1999) "External debt and economic growth in sub-Saharan African countries: An econometric study," Research Paper 90, AERC Research Paper Series. Nairobi, Kenya: African Economic Research Consortium, March.

Iyoha, M. A. (2000) "The sources of economic growth in Nigeria, 1960-1997: A growth accounting exercise," *Nigerian Economic and Financial Review,* Vol. 5, No. 2, December.

James, W. E., S. Naya and G. Meier (eds.) (1987) *Asian Development Economic Success and Policy Lessons,* San Francisco: Institute for Contemporary Studies.

Kenwood, A. G. and A. L. Longheed (1970) *The Growth of the International Economy 1820-1960,* Albany, N.Y.: State University of New York Press.

Kohli, K. N. (1989) "Economic Trends in Asia," fu Seiji Naya *et al.* (eds.), *Lessons in Development: A Comparative Study of Asia and Latin America,* San Francisco: ICEG.

Krueger, A. O. (ed.) (1988) *Development with Trade: LDCs and the International Economy,* San Francisco, California: International Center for Economic Growth.

Kumets, S. (1959) *Six Lectures on Economic Growth,* New York: The Free Press.

Maddison, A. (1970) *Economic Progress and Policy in Developing Countries,* New York: W. W. Norton & Co. Inc.

Mallampally, P. and K. P. Sauvant (1999) "Foreign direct investment in developing countries," *Finance and Development,* March.

Marshall, A. (1959) *Principles of Economics,* 8th ed., London.

Michaely, M. (1977) "Exports and growth: An empirical investigation," *Journal of Development Economics,* Vol. 4, No.1, March.

Naya, S. (1990) *Private Sector Development and Enterprise Reforms in Growing Asian Economies,* San Francisco California: International Centre for Economic Growth.

Naya, S., M. Urrutia, S. Mark and A. Fuentes (eds.) (1989) *Lessons in Development: A Comparative Study of Asia and Latin America,* San Francisco, California: International Centre for Economic Growth.

Sarel, M. (1997) "Growth and productivity in ASEAN-4 countries," *IMF Working Paper* 97/97, Washington, D. C.: International Monetary Fund.

UNCTAD (1998) *World Investment Report 1998: Trends and Determinants,* New York and Geneva: United Nations.

Weitz, A. and L. Lijane (1998) *External Resource Flows to Developing Countries,* ODS Working Paper 3. New York: United Nations Development Programme.

World Bank (1996) *World Debt Tables: External Finance for Developing Countries Vol.* I *(Analysis and Summary Tables),* Washington, D. C.: The World Bank.

World Bank (1998) *African Development Indicators: 1998/99,* Washington, D. C.: World Bank.

Young, A. (1995) "The tyranny of numbers: confronting the statistical realities of the East Asian growth experience," *Quarterly Journal of Economics,* 110, 3, August.

2

Nature and meaning of globalization

– Ernest Aiyedun

Introduction

Globalization connotes a presence, the process of "making global", "being present world wide" "at the world stage," or "global arena". These imply visibility, immediacy, or availability. Thus an issue, object, value(s), institutions, or practices is globalized if either through commerce, production, consumption, politics and information technology it is visible or considered relevant in global centres.

Globalization entails universalization whereby the object, practices or even values transcends geo-political boundaries, penetrating the hitherto sovereign nation-state and impacting the orientation and value system of the people. It is from this vantage that we could speak of globalization of human rights, sustainable development, issues of environment, rule of law, democracy and good governance. Thus, it is from this perspective that one could understand the swift reaction of Commonwealth of nations, the European Union, the United Nations and the United States against the authoritarian regime of the late General Sani Abacha following the execution of Ken-Saro Wiwa and eight other Ogoni leaders (Abubakar, 2001).

The failure of the then military junta to respect the provisions of the Harare Declaration on respect for the rule of law, fundamental human rights and good governance earned Nigeria not only a suspension from the Commonwealth but isolation and sanctions from its erstwhile western partners. The foregoing illustrates one dimension of the process of globalization from the perspective of universalization of value systems and its implications for the New International Order.

Another usage of the concept of globalization emphasizes the element of power relations among actors either at the economic, political or sociocultural levels. From this perspective, globalization entails a "constructionist" as well as recompositionist notion -a process of making or remaking of the world and the existence of a system or structure ranging from an integrated, yet expanding, capitalist market, a world of information and communication order, or a structured world political order, or a structured world political order. Thus within this perspective, we could speak of element or structures of domination, polarization, inequalities, marginalisation and asymmetry (Abubakar, 2001).

Globalization, therefore, implies global culture and civilization, global economy, and the expression of the global political and military orders. From the foregoing, it is obvious that the concept of globalization has diverse usage, but in the context of this chapter, the focus is on the African perspective on global financial crisis. In other words, the discussion of knowledge economics in developing world must necessarily be linked with the processes of globalization because the very concepts, paradigms and theoretical perspectives that we use in understanding the Third World socio-economic and political terrain are essentially imported. For this reason, it is alarmingly losing its capacity to think for itself, and increasingly falling to "policy dependence syndrome" or dependence on externally generated and externally driven policies. This, in-turn, has entrenched the dominance of expatriate personnel in policy-making and policy implementation in the Third World (Kagwanja, 1997).

There had been gross under funding of the education sector in the past two decades in Nigeria. The meagre resources that actually went into the system were quite often mismanaged, misapplied, or misappropriated by corrupt University administrators (Jega, 1994).

This chapter reviews recent trends in increasing linkages among countries or the deeper integration of the world economy by trade, finance, direct investment, technology, knowledge, health, environmental concerns, military, religion, political ideology, and the encouragement of regionalism. It examines expanding financial turmoil, which has been triggered by the Asian crisis, and its impact on African countries. The chapter also explores the main lessons and policy implications for African countries. Following this introduction, section 2 gives a brief discussion of the qualitative and quantitative impact of Asian crisis on African countries. Section 3 highlights the challenges posed by the transformation in the global economy as a result of developments in information technology and worldwide adoption of policy of deregulation. Section 4 presents African perspective of globalization knowledge in the twenty-first century. Finally section 5 provides the main lessons, policy implications and conclusion.

Impact of the Asian financial crisis on Africa

The developing countries of Africa can make a major difference in global financial system if and when they have adequate control over their financial requirements. The global financial system has witnessed rapid growth and substantial structural change during the last decade leading to globalization of financial markets. The integration of financial markets has accentuated the rapid flow of capital across borders as well as magnified the contagious effects of financial crisis with wide implications for transmission of financial policies on the domestic economy and internationally. The recent financial crisis, which originated in East and South East Asia (hereafter Asia) and transformed into a global crisis is a case in point.

The present financial crisis, which originated in East Asia, has been triggered by the devaluation of the Thai currency in July 1997. This situation was accentuated when Malaysia took a snap decision to ban short selling -the sale of a borrowed stock in anticipation of buying it back later at a cheaper price. The ban on short selling caused some investors to sell up all together and leave the market. Consequently, the Malaysian currency plunged to new all-time low, prompting fresh attacks on East Asian currencies. A direct result of the crisis is the deep economic recession in the region affecting many Asian economies, particularly Indonesia, South Korea, Thailand and Malaysia. Japan, the leading economy in the region and the World's second largest economy, is experiencing its worst recession since World War II. The onset of the Asian crisis seems to have taken everybody by surprise because the Asian countries that were hit by the crisis had been among the most successful in sustaining high rates of economic growth, keeping high saving and investment rates and improving the quality of life of their citizens. However, the emerging consensus is that the Asian crisis is a hybrid of structural and policy distortions (macro-and micro-economic) in the affected economies.

Table 1: Largest export items from Africa and Asia

Africa exports	*1990 (%)*	*1996 (%)*
Total Africa exports	100.0	100.0
Mineral fuels and related materials	44.6	38.0
Food, beverages and tobacco	16.7	18.9
Crude materials (excluding fuels) oils, fats	15.0	17.5
Chemicals	11.7	12.6
Other manufactured goods	9.2	10.4
Machinery and transport equipment	2.5	2.3

The impact of the crisis on African countries was mainly transmitted through declines in export prices and volumes. The low demand for primary commodities induced by the crisis and the large depreciation of Asian currencies appear to have played major roles in depressing commodity prices. With only a few exceptions, the commodities that suffered large price declines are those for which Asia constitutes an important market (e.g. oil and/or those supplied by Asian countries e.g. copper, timber and rubber). In Table 1 it is shown that the effect of the Asia crisis on African exports is majorly felt by mineral fuels and related materials, which constitute 38% of Africa's totals exports to Asia.

African countries encounter solid competition from Asian producers in the markets of primary exports such as cocoa, timber rubber, coffee and tea (Table 2).

Table 2: Competition with Africa in export markets

Commodity	Africa			Asia		
	1970	*1993*	*% change*	*1970*	*1993*	*% change*
Cocoa	80.3	60.1	-20.2	0.4	20.0	19.6
Coffer	24.3	14.3	-10.3	4.9	10.9	6.0
Rubber	7.4	5.6	-1.8	89.1	90.8	1.7
Timber	13.4	7.3	-6.1	43.3	52.5	9.2
Cotton	30.7	17.2	-13.5	16.6	35.6	19.0

As shown in Table 3, the crisis had a large negative effect on the export proceeds of oil exporting country of Algeria (-32.7%) and non-oil exporting country of Ghana (-17.6%) because of decline in world price of gold. Africa's oil-exporting countries, which experienced large deterioration in their terms of trade, especially those that have large shares of their export to the crisis region: Nigeria 12%, Algeria 9.7% and Libya 9.5% were the most affected. For the continent as a whole, export proceeds declined by 9.5% between 1997 and 1998. This was the product of a 7% decline in export prices and a 2.5% decline in volume of exports. The crisis has cost Africa about US$2 billion higher than the annual average flow of Foreign Direct Investment in recent years. The crisis was majorly caused by private capital to private borrowers. Most of the debt was due to private companies and banks and not to the government as in the case of Mexico's in 1994–1995 or African crisis in the 1980s. For the majority of African countries where the inflow of private capital is small and where public debt is dominant, the traditional risk management policies, such as adopting realistic exchange rates and reducing government deficits and inflation rate should continue to be major policy tools to prevent financial crisis. However, as the role of private capital increases the design of macroeconomic policies would need to heed lessons emerging from Asia.

Table 3: The effect on exports of individual African countries (US$ billion)

African countries	Before crisis (A)	After crisis (B)	B-A Effect	B-A/A x 100 Effect
Nigeria	14.364	*16.910*	2.545	17.7
Ghana	2.21	1.665	-0.356	-17.6
Ivory Coast	3.979	5.346	1.367	34.4
Cameroon	1.415	1.962	0.547	38.7
Libya	12.344	12.375	0.03 1	0.3

African countries	Before crisis (A)	After crisis (B)	B-A Effect	B-A/A x 100 Effect
Kenya	1.478	2.22	0.544	36.8
Zimbabwe	2.137	2.227	0.090	4.2
South Africa	29.745	28.534	-1.211	-4.1
Algeria	15.388	10.351	-5.037	-32.7
Morocco	6.699	8.15	-1.451	21.7

One basic lesson is that careful sequencing of domestic and external liberalization is needed. This can be achieved through lifting restrictions on the capital account, especially on the more volatile capital flows, only after the domestic financial sector has been strengthened with adequate regulatory and supervisory institutions. This is particularly true because the Asian crisis has shown that reserves, even at very high levels, can be quickly depleted given the scale and volatility of short-term capital flows.

Challenges of globalization through information technology

Some of the topical issues posing serious challenges to policy makers are advances in technology for increasing globalization. Perhaps, the sector that has been most radically affected by these developments is the financial sector. Advances in information technology, in particular, have changed the scope, pace, range as well as procedure of financial services delivery worldwide. The opportunities in developing countries are still restricted because of the stage of development of these economies.

Technological barriers to commerce have fallen as transportation and communication costs have plummeted. Man-made barriers such as tariffs, indigenization policies, exchange rate fluctuations, shock in loans domestically or externally and transparency level have been drastically low. These changes, in addition to the rapid industrialization of the developing world particularly the emerging Asian economies have influenced international economic system and made it more global in nature.

Many countries around the world are investing huge sums of money in factories and other facilities in other countries. Financial market reforms combined with new information technologies enable entrepreneurs in various countries to exchange huge amounts of stocks, bonds and currencies on a daily basis. It is estimated that over ₦100.00 trillion is traded daily in a global foreign exchange market that never closes -while the market is closing in New York, it is opening in Japan and the economic life never sleeps (Okonkwo and Afolabi, 1998). In addition, the Society for Worldwide Interbank Financial Telecommunications (SWIFT), made possible by advances in information technology and to which some African financial institutions have acquired membership, has facilitated inter-financial institution transactions across the globe.

In spite of the numerous benefits derivable from the current wave of innovation, liberalization, deregulation and globalization which have transformed the contours of the financial services industry worldwide, the development poses many challenges to the regulators/supervisors/operators as well as to the economy in the area of ensuring the stability of the financial system. For instance, with globalization, there is bound to be an increasing competition as well as risk exposures in the financial institutions, which no doubt, poses series of challenges to all the stakeholders. Also, the openness of an economy to international capital markets makes it more exposed to shocks originating from abroad.

Challenges to regulatory/supervisory agencies

The main challenge of globalization facing the financial sector regulators/ supervisors has remained that of how to evolve a regime of supervision that will be efficient, effective, up-to-date and relevant to the ever-changing complexities of modern banking and finance. As a result of globalization, the stability of the financial system may be threatened. For instance, greater market liberalization and internationalization go hand in hand with greater risk of potential disruptions, which originate in or are transmitted through financial markets. More open and competitive markets can develop dynamics of their own and are subject to temporary fluctuations. Heightened competitive pressures, which squeeze profit margins, could lead them to pursue riskier strategies, increasing the possibility of failure. In such circumstances, the regulators/supervisors have as their primary responsibility the maintenance of financial stability, which may be threatened by the increased competitive pressures, brought about by globalization. There is, therefore, the need to take proactive measures in the form of overhauling the existing supervisory framework to address the problem.

Challenges to the operators of globalization

Globalization poses various challenges to operators. One of such challenges is the lack of the required degree of sophistication on the part of the managers of most of our financial institutions to match those of their counterpart in the developed countries. There is also the challenge posed by the inferior levels of technological development as reflected in the low level or even the complete absence of computerization in most of the financial institutions operating in many developing countries, and of particular concern is the position of many banks in the African continent.

Challenges to the economy

As a result of globalization, cross-country capital flows are growing rapidly, and domestic systems are consequently increasingly exposed to shocks emanating from abroad. Since across-border financial flows tend to be more volatile than domestic flows especially equity flows, such flows heighten the risk of financial crisis in many developing economies. Foreign direct investments, for example cannot be relied upon for medium term balance of payments support because it tends to give rise to high profit repatriation and causes high distortions in the host country's economy, which are capable of eroding the benefits. The competitive pressures generated by international financial integration stimulate the pursuit of riskiest strategies that could increase the possibility of distortions as well as the failures in the financial industry.

The greater exposure of developing economies to external shocks inherent in globalization (i.e. global financial integration) raises a number of critical issues such as capital flight, that may be associated with exchange rate and interest rate changes as well as strong capital inflows, which pose new challenges of macro-economic management of the economy. Strong capital inflows reduce host country's policy maker's room for manoeuvre and the external creditors tolerance for poor performance. In particular, such capital flows pose a great dilemma for monetary as well as exchange rate policies. In order to stem inflationary pressures arising from large capital inflows for example, the monetary authority may adopt a tight money policy but this can only be done at the risk of a vicious circle of higher interest rates and a tendency for further inflow. Under the same situation, revaluation of the exchange rate may be required to maintain balance-of-payments stability but again this raises the problem of erosion of the competitiveness of host country's exports, while favouring import activities. Furthermore, as a result of poor technological development in developing economies as well as weak managerial know- how, these economies run the risk of marginalisation from globalization. The challenges poses here include, the problems of adverse terms of trade movement, erosion of commercial preferences for Africa in international trade relations, among others.

African perspective of globalization

Knowledge in the twenty-first century African intellectuals are in crisis not only because of the loss of a sense of history but also the absence of a coherent organisational and conceptual clarity vis-à-vis their mission and vision. One could, for example, ask what are the basic objectives of Nigeria participating in international economic order? To what extent is globalization relevant in addressing Nigeria's problems of underdevelopment, democracy and good governance? What has been the role of African intellectuals in the resolution of the continent's numerous socio-economic and political problems? To what extent does the process of globalization affect African scholars and the future of the continent? How has the discipline of Economics been able to address the issues on how to reduce economic dependence, improve domestic production, control inflation, increase demand for Africa's exports, intensify price competition with Africa exports, reduce Africa's import costs, increase access to capital markets, reduce level of indebtedness, unemployment and poverty, etc. Political scientists should address the perennial problems of lack of good governance and political instability in Africa. Sociologists should address how to tackle the problems of violence, social conflicts, etc. Military experts, engineers, health experts, administrators, etc should address how to be less dependent on sourcing expertise and materials from abroad. To do otherwise is to abdicate responsibility to outsiders.

African scholars have not done much in terms of giving relevant policy-advise to their leaders. Of course, there could be the excuse that they have not been invited or the advice was discarded. However, the literature shows that many African. Scholars, both retired and those still on active service, have been involved in strategies planning, project implementation and advisory positions, especially during undemocratic regimes in Africa. Scholars subverted democracy though sycophancy. They used their skills to turn from serving the cause of democracy, rule of law and good governance, into perpetuating authoritarianism, corruption, lawlessness and abuse of fundamental human rights.

What Africa needs in this twenty-first century to ensure active participation in the current globalization exercise are the organic intellectuals rather than the hitherto inorganic or so called great intellectuals by the western powers. While the great Professors are direct agents of the dominant class and its ideological organizers, the organic intellectuals usually identify with the masses that are the majority, in their struggles for social justice, equality, and rule of law, transparency and discipline.

Since the twentieth century will essentially be the millennium of technology, information, and knowledge, the present African Scholars on ground suggests a need for re-orientation for the necessary leadership for teaching and research development in the global competition.

Africa's dependence on leading western countries such as the United States, Britain, France, and Germany for the importation of goods and services as well as high-technology indicates that the continent has been firmly entrenched in the global capitalist system. With collapsed infrastructures in health, education, transportation, water supply, electricity, communications, etc., coupled with the phenomena of "brain drain", Africa seems to be marginalized in the contemporary globalized world.

Globalization also encourages the gradual erosion of sovereignty and autonomy by nations. Hitherto political issues such as respect for the rule of law, elections and transparency in governance that were seen as domestic or internal affairs of sovereign states are now under the watchful eyes of western countries, the United Nations as well as the political conditionalities which have become the instrument for enforcing compliance. Globalization will undermine or eliminate the role of Africa in defining the priorities of national development. The process of globalization is therefore still about exploitation, accumulation, inequality and capitalist expansion (Ake, 1996). The ability of African governments to regulate their economies will be further eroded by the rules of the World Trade Organisation (WTO) which tend to consolidate the existing international division of labour which confines Africa to a role of supplier of raw materials and commodities and consumer of manufactured goods from developed countries.

The reduction in funding of education in Africa, further deteriorating the existing inadequate infrastructure, research, teaching as well as intensification of brain drain, has forced some African states to go a borrowing from those International Financial Institutions, irrespective of the attached conditionalities. This has some adverse consequences on Africa, which we must all watch out for.

Main lessons: policy implications and conclusion

The process of globalization which entails the expansion of capital and market forces majorly from developed to developing nations, brings along with it harsh socio-economic conditions for the people of Africa. For Africa to be an effective actor in the new globalization, major structural changes must be put in place.

Asia's crisis was triggered by private and not sovereign debts. For the majority of African countries where the inflow of private capital is small and where public debt is dominant, the traditional risk management policies such as adopting realistic exchange rates and reducing government deficits and inflation rates, should be their major concern. Financial crises are more likely in liberalized financial systems. Careful sequencing of domestic and external liberalization is needed, as restriction on the capital account, especially on the more volatile capital flows should be lifted only after domestic financial sector has been strengthened with adequate regulatory and supervisory institutions. Governance issues, which relate to good and transparent management of a country or corporation, have come to playa significant role in the aftermath of the Asian crisis. Part of the problems faced by Asian countries was a reflection of a state-directed capitalism, which included political patronage and nepotism. At the corporate level, it is important that government officials follow generally accepted accounting practices, and banks could seize the collateral backing on loan.

While the ability of developing countries of Africa in taking full advantage offered by the information technology-induced globalization is severely restricted by the stage of development of these African states, this chapter has indicated that the development has transformed the scope, range, pace and the procedure of financial services delivery in these countries despite the fact that they are still developing economies. The 'effects of the development on Africa's financial system have come in the form of cost reduction, enhanced speed at carrying out financial activities, introduction of many computer aided products, improvement in the transactions in the nation's capital market and opportunity to access the global market for enhancing capital base by some financial firms.

In spite of the numerous benefits that can be derived from globalization induced by advances in information technology, the chapter noted that the development poses many challenges to the regulators/supervisors, the operators in the financial market and the economy as a whole. The current wave of innovation, liberalization, deregulation and globalization poses a threat to the stability of a nation's financial system with its attendant negative consequences on the overall economy. In order to avert or at least minimise the dangers posed by this development, there is the need for the regulators/supervisors to evolve a regime of supervision that will be efficient, effective, up-to-date and relevant to the ever-changing complexities of modern banking and finance. On the part of operators, there is the need for the development of management strategies that would enable them to identify all such risks as environmental risks, process risks and operational risks that are normally associated with globalization activities. For the economy as a whole, the current efforts at deregulation, privatization and liberalization, under a democratic setting, should be cautiously pursued, with a human face, to enable the economy benefit optimally from opportunities offered by technology-induced globalization.

The deterioration in the educational sector, especially in terms of infrastructures, and conditions of intellectuals, diminished the possibilities of African scholars playing a fundamental role in the repositioning of the continent in the twenty-first century. The chapter also pointed out that intellectuals who are supposed to give policy relevant advice have for the past two decades, become sycophants in the service of military dictators. The erosion of the legitimacy of the state arising from its failure to meet the basic needs of the populace has been an important dimension in the underdevelopment of Africa.

The process of repositioning or reconstruction of the African State to serve the interests of the majority can be done through mass qualitative education, open access to scientific research, findings, development of indigenous (traditional) institutions, mobilization and full involvement of the people in the decision-making process. Ownership like empowerment cannot be given. It must be earned the hard way.

References

Abubakar, D. (2001) "Globalization, Social Sciences and Nigeria in the 21st Century," *Newscience of Social Science Academy of Nigeria*, Vol. 4 No.1 March.

Ake, C. (1992) "The New World Order: A View from the South," Malthouse Press for CASS, Lagos.

Ake, C. (1996) "Democracy and Development in Africa" The Brookings Institution, Washington D.C.

Dembele, D.M. (1998) "Africa in the Twenty-first Century," *CODESRIA Bulletin*, No. 1.

Hussain, M.N.K. Mlambo and T. Oshikoya (1999) "Global Financial Crisis: An African Perspective," *African Development Review* Vol. 11, No.2.

Ihonvbere, J. O. (1996) "Africa and the New Globalization: Challenges and Options for the Future," In H.F. Didsbury, Jr. (ed.) *Future Vision: Ideas Insights. and Strategies,* Maryland.

Jega, A.M. (1994) "Nigerian Academics under Military Rule," Department of Political Science, University of Stockholm.

Kagwanja, P.M. (1997) "Post-Industrialism and Knowledge Production: African Intellectuals in the New International Division of Labour," *CODESRIA Bulletin*, No.3.

Manheim, M. (1993) "Integrating Global Organisations Through Task/Team Support Systems," in Linda M.H. ed. *Global Networks: Computers and International Communication*, The MIT Press Massachusetts, Cambridge.

Lee Hamilton (1997) "Globalization of the Economy," *Washington Report* Vol. XXXII, No.44.

Okonkwo, R. K. and J.A. Afolabi (1998) "The Challenges of Information Technology and Globalization For The Nigerian Financial System," *NDIC Quarterly*, Vol. 8, No. 5.

Opero, J.E. (1996) "The Challenges of Globalization," Being remarks given at the World Economic Development Congress, Washington D.C.

Yoshino, M.Y. and U.S. Rangan (1995) *Strategic Alliances: An Entrepreneurial Approach to Globalization*, Harvard Business School Press, Boston.

3

The democracy movement and globalization: Nigeria in perspective

– Solomon O. Ogbu

Introduction

Democracy and globalization dominate world affairs today. The two phenomena now have far-reaching impacts on the economies and social existence of most nations of the world. But how does Nigeria fit into these democratic and global visionary trends?

There has been a lot of democratic experiments in the chequered political history of Nigeria, a history that is punctuated with a long spell of military rule characterized by systematic and ruthless assaults on the ideals of democracy. But like a wounded lion, a number of pro-democracy activists unperturbed by the repressive measures of the military, struggled relentlessly until the military finally handed over power to a democratically elected government on May 29, 1999. The task before the leadership of the country now is to consolidate the gains of democracy in order to ensure fundamental human rights, political stability and sustainable economic development.

Globalization refers to the profound socio-economic and technological interactions that now pervade the entire world. The rapid and constant networks of communication among all peoples of the world have shrunk the world into a "global village". Globalization has brought in its trail immense benefits to the international community, but it has also impacted negatively on certain sections of the international community. Under the present international capitalist system, the benefits of globalization accrue mainly to the developed countries while the poor countries of the South remain vulnerable to its negative impacts.

Nigeria needs a leadership that can harness and utilise judiciously the country's abundant human and natural resources to enhance her capacity to compete with the active actors in the global system. In this way, she will be able to have a fair share of the benefits of globalization.

This chapter underscores the need for Nigeria to put her "house" in order so that she can also reap the benefits of globalization. This requires a deliberate policy on the part of government to train and re-train the country's human resources, expand infrastructure and enhance her economic power so that she can rise to the challenges of globalization in the twenty-first century.

The chapter is divided into five sections. Section 1 is the introduction, which highlights the salient issues involved in the subject matter. Section 2 discusses democracy and the Nigerian democratic experience. Section 3 presents a critical analysis of globalization and the rest of the Third World. Section 4 consists of recommendations; and section 5 contains the concluding remarks.

Democracy and the Nigerian democratic experience

The term 'democracy' is pregnant with meanings. It is a popular expression among people, particularly statesmen and political leaders who, lay claims to democratic governance regardless of the type of government they are running. Consequently, virtually all the definitions of democracy given by different scholars and political actors over the years are value-laden and nebulous in that the definitions are grounded on their subjective individual perceptions of democracy relative to the ethical and ideological leanings of their respective societies.

Today, democracy has certainly developed beyond its direct practice in the Greek city-state of Athens upon which it was defined by Abraham Lincoln as "government of the people for the people and by the people". Accordingly, most definitions of democracy at the present time take cognisance of the representative nature of modern democracy. Thus Black (1979:388) has defined democracy as "that form of government in which the sovereign power resides in and is exercised by the whole body of free citizens directly or indirectly through a system of representation as distinguished from a monarchy, aristocracy, or oligarchy."

The definition given by Professor L. M. Lipset is particularly illuminating in that it sufficiently highlights the fundamental features of the representative democracy that is now in vogue in the world:

> A political system which supplies regular constitutional opportunities for changing the governing officials and a social mechanism which permits the largest possible part of the population to influence major decisions by choosing from contenders of political officers.

Essentially, democracy is founded on the popular will of the people and this is expressed at periodic elections. Thus, "the primary criterion for democracy is therefore an equitable and open competition for votes between and among political parties without government manipulation, harassment or restrictions of opposition parties" (Chichana, 1998: 39). Democracy is a system of choice by the electorate who constitutes the political sovereign. It originated from Athens, a Greek city-state, and has become a form of government universally accepted as the best in the modern world. The application of the principles of democracy may vary slightly from society to society due to peculiar historical and social circumstances, but the culture and essential elements of democracy remain basically the same all over the world. These include:

(1) The centrality of the people in the determination of what Harold Lasswell termed "who gets what, when and how?"

(2) Free and fair elections and periodic change of government; and

(3) Independent judiciary; guaranteeing of fundamental human rights and freedoms as well as the rule of law.

Modern democracy can be conceptualised in three inter-related ways (Nzongola-Vtalaja, 2001:20). These are:

(a) Democracy as a moral imperative;

(b) Democracy as a social process; and

(c) Democracy as a political practice.

Democracy as a moral imperative relates to the quest for a congenial atmosphere for men to develop their potentials to the fullest and have good life. To this end, Aristotle had said that "for the sake of good life" the establishment of democratic form of good is imperative in human society. In the same vein, Thomas Hobbes emphasised that an effective and responsible form of government is a necessary condition for men to exhibit their inherent virtues and also demonstrate the law of nature - modesty, justice, mercy, and equity. Indeed, it is only under a peaceful and stable democratic system that men can enjoy their freedoms, pursue their aspirations and build an egalitarian society. Any government that claims to be democratic must demonstrate the moral obligation to facilitate the attainment of these aspirations. No doubt, there is a positive correlation between peace, democracy, and national development.

Democracy as a social process is a mechanism for protecting and promoting the fundamental human rights and civil liberties of citizens. Experiences all over the world have shown unequivocally that democracy is the form of government that best guarantees the inalienable rights and liberties of citizens. In a democratic system, these rights are eloquently written into the constitution for avoidance of doubt, and they are legally and morally binding on government to guarantee. The adoption and consolidation of democracy in most parts of the world today is a reaction to the failure of the military and other forms of authoritarian governments to guarantee these basic social needs.

As a political practice, democracy is a mode of governance based on the principles of the sovereignty of the people, the rule of law, accountability, participation, and periodic change of government. The existence of political institutions such as the executive, the legislature, the judiciary as well as the armed forces, each of which is charged with specific political functions is a manifestation of the existence of a national government in a society.

Democracy has clearly emerged as the form of government that most significantly takes cognisance of the interests and welfare of the masses. Among other things, it provides social opportunities likely to enhance the capabilities of individuals to develop their potentials. For the common man, this means increasing his capacity to overcome poverty, protest against unemployment and social exclusion, and increase the ability to take advantage of the favourable economic environment to improve his standard of living. Politically, even the poor are empowered in a democratic system. This means that they are included in the concept of power-sharing in such a way that they take part in the development process through a system of self-management akin to the now famous model of the Brazilian city of Porto Alegre, where neighbourhood residents can, through a "participatory budget" engage in determining how municipal funds are allocated to their development needs. This is illustrative of the agitation for resource control by some states in Nigeria.

All the above symbolises the beauty of democracy, and it is the passion and struggle to embrace this beauty that has today made democracy a worldwide movement. The major defects in democracy are the inability of the majority of citizens to understand the extremely difficult and complicated issues of social and economic policies involved in modern government, the constant danger of their being deluded by unscrupulous politicians and leaders to support policies that are irrational, their poor sense of judgement in deciding who to vote for, and their ignorance and general gullibility.

The Nigerian democratic experience

Nigeria has not been left out in what has become a world-wide drive towards establishing and consolidating a viable democratic system. In fact, like everywhere else, the western (democratic) wind is blowing soothingly over the Eastern (socialist) wind in Nigeria; that is, the pervasive waves of the western liberal democracy have every where, including Nigeria, swept away all vestiges of the conservative socialist system.

On becoming independent on October 1, 1960 Nigeria adopted the parliamentary democracy borrowed from her departing British colonial masters. Unfortunately, the nascent democracy of the First Republic was short-lived as it was terminated by the military on January 15, 1966 in a bloody coup d'etat after only six years of its introduction. This was followed by 19 years of military dictatorship during which the ideals of democracy were trampled upon with ruthless abandon.

Democracy, based on the American presidential system, was established in 1979. This ushered in the Second Republic. It paved the way for the reemergence of the culture of democracy and hence of the enthronement of fundamental human rights and the rule of law. The federal system made up of three tiers of government - the federal, the state, and the local government levels - was firmly in place. The 1979 Federal Constitution of Nigeria, which was operated by the then federal government, provided for three legislative lists – the exclusive list, the concurrent list, and the residual list.

Under the arrangement, the NPN-controlled federal government had exclusive legislative power in respect of matters on the exclusive list. Such matters included defence, currency, and foreign affairs. The concurrent list contained such matters as education, roads, health, and water resources upon which both the federal government and the state governments could legislate. The decision of the federal government prevailed in respect of any conflict between the federal government and any of the state governments on any of the matters contained on the list. Such miscellaneous things as primary education, naming of streets, and licensing of things like bicycles, market stalls, etc were left for the local government system.

The Second Republic was overthrown by the military on December 31, 1983, and this again plunged the country into another protracted period of military interregnum characterised by yet another round of draconian decrees and insensitivity to democratic norms and values. Determined attempts made in 1993 and in 1998 to return the country to civil rule failed until 1999, when the military finally bowed out of the corridors of power.

Table 1: Comparison, in terms of number of years in power, between civilian and military rule in Nigeria

Years	Period	Type of regime	No. years in office
1960-1966	01/10/60-15/01/66	Civilian	06
1966-1979	15/01/66-01/10/79	Military	13
1979-1983	01/10/79-31/12/83	Civilian	04
1983-1999	31/12/83-29/05/99	Military	16
1999-present (2001)	29/09/99-to date	Civilian	02

Total number of years of military rule: 29 (70.73%)
Total number of years of civilian rule: 12 (29:27%)

Source: Federal Ministry of Information, Nigeria (1999).

On the whole, the Nigerian experience at democratisation was until May, 1999 traumatic and horrendous. The military officers who had become accustomed to the exercise of political power and all the good things associated with it severally aborted and frustrated the efforts of patriotic Nigerians to return the country to democratic governance. Of the forty-seven years (by the year

2007) of Nigeria's existence as an independent nation, the military were in power for a total of twenty-nine years.

However, it would not be true to assert that the military in all their years in power did not make any positive impact on the society. In the first place, they came to power ostensibly to put an end to monumental corruption, ineptitude, and nepotism that had characterised the civilian administrations that they overthrew. As a corrective regime, the military, while in power in Nigeria, made significant contributions in the areas of road construction and rehabilitation, education (especially the establishment of many more universities), the re-location of the federal capital from the over-crowded and chaotic city of Lagos to a more spacious location, Abuja. It is to their credit that the military under General Babangida introduced the structural adjustment programme (SAP) and other laudable economic measures to revamp the ailing economy.

The future of democracy in Nigeria

The future of democracy in Nigeria depends largely on the capacity of the country to eliminate all the problems that had bedevilled the establishment and consolidation of democracy in the country. One of the most formidable of these problems relates to the insatiable lust of the Nigerian military for political power. To this extent, any attempt to consolidate democracy in the society must necessarily proceed from discouraging the military from embarking on another direct intervention in the body politic of the country. The military should be made to subscribe to the notion of civilian supremacy in the political life of any nation, and to concentrate on performing their professional roles, particularly the defence of the territorial integrity of the nation.

Two, paradoxically the country's politicians are their own enemy. Their greed, inefficiency, and gross mismanagement of the country's scarce resources while in power had provided the alibi for the military to seize power from them a couple of times. Thus, the stability of our long-sought for and found democracy depends by and large on the performance of the country's civilian leaders; credible performance enhances the legitimacy of any civilian government. During the Second Republic, for example, ministers, governors, and other highly placed politicians, were wallowing in conspicuous consumption while the masses where languishing in abject poverty. Such an intolerable situation can prompt the military to intervene anywhere in the world.

Three, nepotism and tribalism constitute the bane of Nigerian politics. For example, different sections of the country have consistently complained about allocation injustices in the appointment of government functionaries, in the distribution of power and other vital resources among the six geo-political zones, and in leadership succession at the national level. The zoning formula of the People's Democratic Party (PDP) could go a long way in dealing with these problems, but the fear is that the formula may not stand the test of time, more so as the PDP is already engulfed in a serious intra-party crisis that threatens its unity and solidarity.

Four, vigorous political education and enlightenment must be undertaken by government to acquaint the civil society with the benefits of democracy. This is the only way to win and sustain the support of the electorate, which constitutes the political sovereign, and on whom political stability depends.

Five, institutional deficiency or weakness poses a serious threat to the consolidation of democracy in the country. In the present Fourth Republic, the political parties and the National Assembly that are the principal institutions of the democratic system are faced with formidable centrifugal forces. All the three-registered parties- the PDP, the APP, and the AD - are suffering from deep internal crises that have severely weakened their strength and legitimacy. The National Assembly has from the inception of the Fourth Republic engaged the Presidency in a running battle for power and supremacy.

All this has dire implications for the country's nascent democracy, and it makes a mockery of our democratic experiment in the eyes of the international community. The political class must put its "house" in order for the hard won democracy to be sustained in the country.

Nigeria and globalization

Globalization

Globalization is the interdependence among nations that has more than ever before become noticeably profound and multifaceted. Globalization is not a new phenomenon; it has been evolving over the decades. At its early stages, it simply meant the internationalisation of trade and national economies.

Today, globalization has gone beyond the economic nexus among nations. For example, political and diplomatic relations among nations have become more pronounced, movement of persons as well as goods and services across national boundaries is now much easier, communication between one country and another has become greatly enhanced. All of these things are facilitated by modern means of communication and technology such as the cellular phone, Internet links, and multimedia networks.

It is against this background that Robinson (1998:1) has defined globalization as the "movement of goods, services, and especially financial assets and information across national boundaries in the quest for international diversification of investment portfolios." For Wayem (1998:1) globalization is characterised by the "rapid growth of international trade and capital flows; the increasing importance of services in both trade and foreign direct investment; the global integration of production processing; and the institutional harmonisation among countries with regard to trade, tax and investment policies as well as other regulations, and an increasing tendency towards the liberalisation of international trade."

Thus, "globalization is a process integrating not just the economies but cultures, technologies and governance" (Sheidu, 2001:3). Needless to say, the developed capitalist countries constitute the driving force of the phenomenon of globalization as it provides them with a leeway to further advance their economic and imperialist penetration of the less developed countries. For example, it provides the multinational corporations owned by the developed world with a fertile ground to intensity their exploitative economic activity in the less developed countries since these countries are economically ill-equipped and ill-prepared to cope with the unhealthy competition posed by them (the developed counties). In essence, globalization sharpens the dichotomy and the unequal exchange between the rich North and the poor South thereby polarising the world into two diametrically opposed classes.

However, globalization portends to re-awaken the less developed countries to brace up with the challenges of rapid economic development and social progress. It has also enhanced liberal international trade from which the less developed countries can benefit immensely once they put their "houses" in order.

Nigeria in perspective

Ordinarily, one would say that the emergent "global village" is a welcome development for Nigeria and the rest of the world, particularly the third world that needs the co-operation and assistance of the developed world for human and material development. Indeed, Nigeria stands to reap the benefits of globalization if she can harness and judiciously utilise the abundant natural and human resources at her disposal so as to be able to compete with other active actors in the global system. Globalization entails a great deal of competition and it is only those actors that have been able to put their act together that can cope with the global competition for wealth acquisition, for viable export markets, and even for power and supremacy.

In Nigeria, manpower development that is crucial for economic and industrial development is not receiving the attention it deserves from government. Consequently, the skill and technical expertise required to put the country on the path of sustainable development are pathetically deficient in the country. The acquisition of technical know-how and the knowledge of new production techniques is a *sine qua non* for technological development. The earlier Nigeria realises that highly skilled manpower is essential for technological development which will in turn put her in a good stead to participate actively in global affairs, the sooner will she begin to benefit from the phenomenon of globalization.

Globalization is facilitated by internet links. Unfortunately, Nigeria's link with the internet is still in its infancy and this is a major constraint to the capacity and ease with which she can reach out to the rest of the world.

For Nigeria to be firmly in contention in the global competition, vigorous efforts must be made to strengthen her connection to the internet. This can be achieved by expanding her media networks and satellite communication technology without any further delay.

The country's heavy indebtedness to the western powers and the Bretton Woods institutions – the International Monetary Fund (IMF) and the World Bank – controlled also by the western powers has perpetually put Nigeria and other debtor countries in a weak position in the global scheme of things. Globalization contributed immensely to the ease and recklessness with which the loans were obtained from the western powers and their lending agencies. In essence, Nigeria remains subservient to these great powers and this has dire implications both for her sovereign rights and her bargaining power on trade policy issues relating to her national interest. All this has debilitating effect on how much benefit she can derive from the pervasive phenomenon of globalization. The world market has no rules or norms of society behaviour or any form of control mechanism. Thus, globalization is characterised by "survival of the fittest syndrome" which is inimical to the interests of Nigeria and other less developed countries of the world.

The environmental pollution being experienced in Nigeria, particularly in the oil-producing Niger Delta area of the country, is one of the major consequences of globalization for the country. The lives of fish and other aquatic animals and species as well as farm land have been endangered due to the gas flaring and the toxic waste associated with the extraction process of the oil. This is the handiwork of the multinational corporations that have taken advantage of globalization to operate anywhere in the world, particularly in the less developed regions of the world where they have little or no competition from the host countries. The task of the Nigerian government in this regard would be to empower indigenous firms financially to compete with, and possibly take over, the oil sector business and hence the commanding heights of the economy from expatriates. This will strengthen Nigeria's position in the global system.

Concluding remarks

Democracy and globalization are issues that have come to occupy the front seat in the modern world affairs. The world is undergoing rapid transformation in the democratic and globalization processes. The all-crusading western liberal democracy has become a worldwide movement, pervading even what used to be the socialist enclave in Eastern Europe.

Foreign aid and technical assistance from the West and their allies are now tied to democracy. Thus, Nigeria must join the bandwagon of the democracy movement in order to earn for herself a respectable position in the international community. In the present circumstances in the world, democracy is clearly the inevitable option for Nigeria and other countries of the world.

This underscores the need for Nigeria to firmly entrench the principles of democracy and ensure political stability. The political leaders of the country must adopt a new psychological orientation towards politics by endeavouring to serve the nation to the best of their ability rather than pursue parochial interests and personal aggrandisement. The historic statement by John F. Kennedy, a former President of the United States of America, that "Americans should not ask for what the country can do for them but what they can do for her", is instructive to Nigerian political actors.

The immense opportunities for economic and technological development that abound in the "global village" can only be availed of under a stable political system which democracy more than any other form of government provides. At present, it is mostly the developed capitalist countries that enjoy the benefits of globalization while the developing countries are still struggling to get a foothold in the emerging world economic and socio-political order. Globalization is fostered by the capitalist system, a system that favours the bourgeois countries and penalises the developing countries.

In the corollary, for Nigeria to make any meaningful progress in the 21st century she must enhance her economic power to cope with the keen competition that is inherent in globalization. Globalization, like democracy, is irreversible and unavoidable and so everything possible must be done by Nigeria to embrace and benefit from it. In pursuit of economic recovery, and to enhance her capacity to compete in the global economy, Nigeria has joined the bandwagon of other developing countries pursuing development programmes to embark on trade liberalisation, economic deregulation and privatisation of public enterprises as part of her structural adjustment process. In spite of these, "problems such as political and macroeconomic instability, and inconsistency of policies, among others, have militated against success in areas such as the inflow of foreign investment and the diversification of the economy" (Ojo, Folayan: 59). These problems have impacted negatively on the degree of economic recovery and the pace of employment generation over the years in the country.

Recommendations

1. Democracy has been accepted world wide as the form of government that can best guarantee fundamental human rights and liberties and hence of conducive atmosphere for social progress and sustainable development. An enduring culture of democracy and political stability devoid of military intrusion is what Nigeria needs to overcome her internal obstacles to development and bring her into reckoning with the progressive members of the international community.

This will also enhance her capacity to cope with the challenges of globalization in twenty-first century.

2. As a leading power in Africa, it behoves Nigeria to take practical steps towards revamping her economy that had been so badly damaged during the 29 years of military dictatorship. A buoyant economy will go a long way in enhancing her image, status, and competitiveness in the world community.

3. Globalization by its very nature is a significant step forward in the technological and social advancement of mankind. It portends to pull the diverse peoples of the world nearer to themselves to share the mutual benefits of close and intimate interactions. But for Nigeria to fully partake of these benefits she must first of all put her "house" in order-undertake radical economic reforms, train and re-train the manpower needed to enhance her capacity to compete favourably with other nations, and come up with deliberate policy to achieve rapid technological development in the near future. Thus, there is an urgent need for institution and capacity building in the country.

4. An enabling environment for the development of the private sector should be created to enhance economic and infrastructure development. As the engine of growth, the private sector, if encouraged, can amass capital that is needed to boost the economy. A well-intentioned privatisation policy will enable the local business entrepreneurs to take over the commanding heights of the economy from the strangulating clutches of government and foreigners, thereby attuning the economy to the needs of Nigerians and the challenges of globalization.

5. Education is the gateway to knowledge and progress. Knowledge is power! The future of the country depends on the access of the child (the girl child inclusive), and women to good functional education. Thus, all stakeholders in education, especially teachers, should be adequately encouraged and motivated with good remuneration and good working conditions.

6. Rules and a regulatory mechanism or body should be established at the global level to control and check the excessive exploitation of the weak countries in the global co-operation to benefit from one another. The weak countries, including Nigeria, that have not been able to benefit appreciably from the phenomenon of globalization should be legally empowered to control and nationalise, where necessary, multinational corporations in order to check excessive capital flight from the Third World economies. Nigeria should help to champion the campaign for this.

References

Black, H. (1979) *Black's Law Dictionary*, 5th Ed., St. Paul Minn, West Publishing Co.

Chihana, (1998) "Intervention" in Aderinwale and Alabi (eds.), *Democratisation of African Parliaments and Political Parties,* published under the auspices of the World Bank Institute.

Nzongola-Ntalaja (2001) "The Democracy Project in Africa: The Journey so far," *The Nigerian Social Scientist,* Vol.4, No. 1.

Ojo, Folayan (2001) "Profile of Tertiary Graduate Production in Nigeria: An Analysis of Training and Labour Market Gaps," in Ebebe Ukpong (ed.), *Bridging Tertiary Institutions and Labour Market in Nigeria,* Ibadan: National Manpower Board, Nigeria.

Robinson, V. (1998) "African Competitiveness within the Global Economy: The Case of the Lesotho National Development Corporation."

Sheidu, A. (2001) "Globalization and Human Development in Nigeria: Linkages, Implications and Challenges". Being a paper delivered at the 2001 Annual National Conference on social Science Administration in the 21st Century by the Faculty of Social Sciences and Administration, Usman Danfodio University, Sokoto, 22-24 January, 2001.

Section II

Specific issues

4

The social and economic impact of globalization on Nigeria

– Otaki Osana Alanana

Introduction

On the concrete evidence of history, a German philosopher and economist, Karl Marx (1818–1883) wrote at the turn of the nineteenth century that every society is in constant motion. This motion is a reflection of the coexisting social forces.

Consequently, change is propelled. This change can either be qualitative or quantitative. The transition from slavery to feudalism and capitalism results from the presence of social forces (Eaton, 1966; Marx, 1967).

Globalization, although a new social phenomenon, falls within the realms of this change process. And because of the global interrelatedness, dating back to the aforementioned historical periods, Nigeria continues to experience a trickle down effect of whatever positive or negative development in the metropolitan Europe.

This chapter attempts to analyse the social and economic effects of globalization on Nigeria, as a social process. An examination of globalization as an offshoot of imperialism is also made. This stage, it is argued, transcends the stage Nkrumah (1972) described as final and dangerous in the social evolution of capitalist development. Also the chapter addresses some applicable theoretical issues, and concludes by way of suggesting possible remedy to alleviate the major social and economic impact of globalization on Nigeria and her peoples. On this basis, the chapter is structured into four parts. While part one introduces the chapter, the second part discusses some relevant theoretical issues on globalization. Part three, which forms the crux of the chapter discuses, the social and economic impact of globalization. Part four discusses the concluding part of the chapter.

Some theoretical issues

Like any other social construct, globalization as a concept does not have a precise meaning. This concept has been variously defined. Some see it as a new stage in a capitalist development, generally referred to as "late capitalism" (Habernas, 1989, Kidro 1979). It is also defined as the development of social and economic relationship stretching world-wide. As a consequence of this process, many aspects of people's lives are influenced by organizations and social networks located millions of miles away from the societies in which they live (Giddens, 1989). However, the key aspect of the social analysis of globalization is the emergence of a world system, evolving gradually into a single social order. This results from the diffusion of social and economic values beyond the European national frontiers.

This process commenced immediately after the bourgeois revolution in Europe in the nineteenth century. The European markets could not absorb the industrial products as part of the fallout of the bourgeois revolution, in addition to near absence of demand for these products, and partly because the industrial workers who produced the wealth were grossly alienated. There was poor wage structure, and so workers could not afford the goods they helped to produce. As a remedy, the nascent capitalist had to search and acquire a new market frontier to actualize the objective of capitalism. This is what Lenin (1976) and Hobson (1966) referred to as imperialism in its naked form. It exercises external domination, economically and politically. This process has continued to date under the guise of integrating the world into a single system for the mutual benefit of all.

Adopting conquest and subjugation as its traits, imperialism and its twin brother, colonialism, overturned in a brutal manner particularly the social and economic structure of Nigeria and Africa as a whole (Balandier, 1967). For example, imperialism/colonialism set in motion the process of social and economic differentiation between the wealth of Euro-America and the poverty of the less developed societies like Nigeria.

This process of social differentiation has intensified under globalization, with trans-nationals, the major international and business outfits as facilitators. They are actively involved in the decapitalization of Nigeria through under-invoicing, over-invoicing of imports and exports of goods and services under the banner of globalization. Some of the goods are not only substandard, but of dubious value. However, the success of this process is predicated on Europe working in league with the Nigerian government.

Although slavery and colonialism were the forerunners of globalization, they have had a profound demographic and social impact on Nigeria. Families were dislocated and lives were lost in the process. Europe and America have maintained this momentum of exploiting Nigeria's resource through globalization, a new process. For example, both Europe and America have continued to maintain a firm control of the Nigerian economy through their leading position in World Trade Organisation (WTO) in addition to the influence they exert on the trans-national corporations (TNCs) globally. Also, through the terms of trade, which they designed, favourable to themselves (Warren, 1989), the metropolitan capitalist countries further maintain their control over the Nigerian economy.

At each of these historical stages, Nigeria was exploited through unequal exchanges. These periods cover the time of slavery when human beings were reduced to the status of commodity and exchanged with assorted items like mirror, perfume, wine, etc. (Rodney 1972). The pillage of Nigeria continued under the colonial system of production. However, under the colonial system, Nigeria was incorporated into the global capitalist market mainly for the purpose of exploiting Nigeria's mineral and agricultural resources. However, there has been no end to exploitation under the neo-colonial structure, as globalization now takes the centre stage.

The social and economic effect

Globalization has emerged as a social phenomenon to replace the concept of imperialism. The social and economic effects on Nigeria and her people are quite profound. Globalization for example, has induced the manufacture of sophisticated industrial products for global capitalist market. These items include computer hard/soft wares, aircraft, cars, pharmaceutical products, and other household products. Apart from altering the social relations of individuals, the consumption pattern of Nigeria has equally changed, as a response to the influx of these items into the Nigerian markets. By this token, globalization is destructive to indigenous industries, and consequently worsens the dependency status of Nigeria. For example, the diffusion of western technology which culminates in the establishment of consumer oriented industries has further accentuated the production of consumer oriented goods like biscuits, toilet paper, detergent, chewing gum etc for the Nigerian market. Therefore, a situation in which globalization does not encourage the establishment of industries that would produce further machines, is not only counter productive but also destructive and antidevelopment.

Again, with globalization, the transnationals have assumed a much more polycentric posture. The TNCs in car production, namely, Mercedes Benz, Toyota, Peugeot, Nissan, BMW and Rovers for example, produce more than one brand of a car for the global markets, which gives them control over the market. But only few Nigerians can indeed afford these cars, yet the cars and other products are claimed to have been produced for the good use of the people. This therefore contradicts the philosophy of globalization as a process in which the world is being integrated to form a single system. Consequently, the gap between the developed capitalist world and less developed societies like Nigeria continues to widen indefinitely.

In the construction, oil, pharmaceutical, marketing and automobile industries, the TNC subsidiaries have registered their presence in Nigeria. Each of the subsidiaries appropriates surplus for its parent companies located in faraway Europe and America. Their activities in oil and construction industries are not only environmentally unfriendly, but also upset the balance of Nigeria's geological structure. Dominated by the TNCs such as Mobil, Elf, Agip, Gulf, Texaco and Shell, the oil sector of the Nigerian economy offers a good example of continuing control and decapitalization of Nigeria despite Federal Governments 60% equity shares in each of the transnational oil companies. In one of his press briefing, Professor Tam David West, former Minister of Petroleum, observed that crude oil worth over one million naira is daily being illegally lifted out of Nigeria by the TNCs (Abba *et al.*, 1985).

Apart from their active involvement in the oil sector of the economy which has effect on the environment, the TNCs form part of the global network which is directly involved in the decapitalization of Nigeria. Table 1 below clearly emphasizes this systematic exploitation of Nigeria.

But in 1994, the average oil production by the TNCs stood at 2.1M b/d or 3.2% of the total world production. According to *Nigeria Federal Public Expenditure Review,* (March 18, 1996), the Nigerian National Petroleum Corporation (NNPC) produces only a very small fraction, approximately 1% of the crude oil.

Another area in which globalization has had a profound effect on Nigeria is that of food and agricultural production. At the colonial and post colonial periods, Nigeria remains one of the major food suppliers to the west mainly via the influences of agribusiness enterprises (Ake, 1986; Onimode 1985; Abba *et al.*, 1985). Under the colonial system of production, a large number of Nigerians were constrained to engage in agricultural production which did not indeed form part of their staples. At this period producing anything contrary to the metropolitan requirements attracted a punitive measure. Yet the produce were grossly undervalued at the international market. For example, a gallon of palm oil produced in Enugu, Eastern Nigeria, sold for one shilling. The same gallon of palm oil sold for twenty pounds sterling (£20) at the international market. This shows how brazenly profit was pounded out of the Nigeria rural producers (Rodney, 1972).

Table 1: Nigeria: oil production 1965–1986

Oil Co.	Period	No of wells		1986 average
		Production	*Total*	
Mobile, Agip Shell, Texaco Chevron, Elf	1965–1986 Between 1986 to date the oil companies are busy investing heavily on exploration.	1253	2151	1,467,542

Source: Adapted from Ikeja, A. A. (1990)

This situation has persisted to date with Nestle, Cadbury-Schweppes, Food Specialties and Lever Brothers, as major actors in the process of decapitalizing Nigeria. Indeed they handle nearly 60–80% of the global cocoa sales. Lever Brothers control the production and marketing of Margarine/Blue Band and table oils. The prices, research and development, which determine the future of Nigeria as a host country, are determined by their parent companies in New York, London and other parts of Europe. Thus, apart from intensifying poverty through this process, the economy of Nigeria is further inoculated with agrarian crisis. Part of the evidence of this crisis is the rising prices of food items in the Nigerian market. Garri, which hitherto was the cheapest staple of the people, is gradually getting out of the reach of the ordinary people. Table 2 below clearly indicates the rising price of food items as part of the fall out of the agrarian crisis.

Table 2: Average prices index from survey of markets in Lagos, Abuja, Benin, Umuahia, Bauchi, Akure and Kano

No.	Foodstuff	Unit	Price in 1999 (₦)	Price in 2000 (₦)	Price in 2001 (₦)
1.	Garri	Bag/tin	1,000/160	500/200	3,000/480
2.	Rice	Bag/tin	2,200/500	2,600/650	3,200/800
3.	Beans	Bag/tin	4,600/500	5,500/650	7,100/800
4.	Yam	5 big tubers	450	650	1,200
		5 medium tubers	350	550	800
		5 small tubers	150	300	600
5.	Corn	Bag/tin	800/90	1,200/120	3,000/300
6.	Palm Oil	20 litre keg	800	1,000	1,600
7.	Milk	Tin	30	40	60
8.	Sugar	Packet	40	45	60

Source: Survey by Newswatch reporters May 28, 2001

Government's inability to deemphasize agrarian fundamentalism in preference to European products is a factor in this crisis and globalization. For example, over 90% of the products in Nigeria market today is imported. This is because of the open door policy of the Nigerian state and response to globalization. These products include textile and modern building materials, confectionery, tooth pick, detergent, and so on. Although the data on this are not readily available, empirical evidence indicates this.

Because of this response to the global change, the number of millionaires in Nigeria continues to increase while, the economy is at the brink of total collapse. Thus the newest models of Toyota Jeep, Mercedes and even *Tokunbo* become the latest status symbols in Nigeria. On the other hand, the poverty profile of the people continues to appreciate at a geometrical progression as the table below indicates, without a corresponding definite policy statement from the Nigerian state, to alleviate the near hopeless situation.

Also with the increasing level of poverty, as part of the fall out of globalization, ethnic acrimony is stirred. Consequently, the country is at the brink of social, economic and political anarchy.

Globalization has added to the fleet of its information technology, with the Global System for Mobile communication (GSM), (the Mobile Telecommunication Network (MTN), and other ancillary communication systems playing a central role in the process. Originally, the idea of the GSM, a superior protocol for mobile telecommunication services, the MTN and so on, were muted to alleviate the unequal access of average Nigerians to telephone services nation wide, and also to integrate Nigeria into the world system. It is indeed a complete but complex system, details of which cannot be explained here because of time and space constraint. However, the GSM and others have their languages and terminology, which the subscribers must learn and get used to if they are to enjoy the services.

The GSM service is ten years old, the idea is just taking root in Nigeria as part of the globalization process. However, the system is full of contradictions. Its service charges are higher in Nigeria than in any other part of Africa. For example, it would cost a subscriber between ₦19 and ₦45 per minute to reach anywhere in the world, according to *The Guardian on Sunday* newspaper of August 5, 2001. While claiming to alleviate communication problem of the subscribers, it has rather intensified the process of alienation of those the project is designed to serve. Through its representatives such as the Nigerian Telecommunication (NITEL), National Communication Commission (NCC) and Bureau for Public Enterprise (BPE), the Nigerian state charges heavy license fees. In order to reap profit from such heavy investment, the GSM and its system have to transfer the burden to the Nigerian subscribers. The consequence of this is the widening gap between the developed countries and the less developed ones as well as between the rich and the poor at the national and international levels.

Table 3: Nigeria: trend in poverty level 1980–1996

Year	Poverty level (%)	Estimated total population (million)	Population in poverty (million)
1980	28.1	65	17.7
1985	46.3	75	34.7
1992	43.7	91.5	39.2
1996	65.6	102.3	67.1

Source: FOS, National Census Survey (1999)

Apart from the elitist posture the GSM and other products of globalization have assumed, the imperial origin of the whole process leaves much to be desired, as globalization has intensified the process of incorporating Nigeria into the global capitalist market.

Advertisement is another area in which globalization has directly affected the social and economic lives of the people of Nigeria. Globalization is facilitated and capitalism legitimized through advertisement. With television and computer wares which form the integral part of globalization, the Nigerian audience is subjected to the psyche manipulation of the TNCs such as Nestle, Cadbury, Chevron, etc. Nestle, for example, sees a lot of potentials in the young ones, who dare to drink Milo, a food drink of future champion. Yet Milo, according to nutritionist, has far less nutritional value compared to local cereal drinks like *akamu, kunu* and *burukutu.*

Large media corporations operating on a global basis have played a central role in the socio-economic lives of Nigerians. Reuter (UK), HAVAS (France), Associated Press (AP, USA) and TASS (Russia). These agencies are responsible for most of the international news, transmitted live or other wise throughout the world. Information to the Nigeria Television Authority (NTA) and the News Agency of Nigeria (NAN) is now sent via satellite and computer links; and because the agencies have a firm control of the global information order the audience tends to believe the news item whether it is true or not. They also package films and televisions programmes and sell to NTA and large international markets. This process is part of the development of a world information order that is grossly uneven. Thus nearly every Nigerian becomes a passive receiver of information from these news agencies that dominate the world information flow. The foreign films have also had impact on the social lives of the people. Socialization and pattern of social behaviour are some of the aspects that have been affected directly. Foreign films, for instance, transmit to the younger Nigerians the values of the West that consequently alter indigenous values of the people.

Conclusion

This chapter argues that although Nigeria cannot isolate herself from the rapid global change, the multiplier effect of this process is counter productive. Through globalization, the values and creativity of Nigerians are eroded. With globalization, the commercial sex work, which was declining in practice in Nigeria, has been elevated to the status of international trade. The consequence is manifold. The diffusion of foreign values and capital as a result of globalization has not yielded a corresponding benefit to Nigeria. Capital flight has intensified, and Nigerians are gradually being pauperized,

As a remedy, it is suggested that the Nigerian state and her collaborators slow down the pace of globalization. The state and private sector can invest heavily on scientific invention and innovation from which the entire country can benefit. Finally, a genuine programme of self-reliant development can be embarked upon and in a no distant time, Nigeria can call Europe's bluff.

References

Abba, *et al.* (1985): *The Nigerian Economics Crisis: Causes and Solution,* Zaria: ASUU
Ake, C. (1985): *The Political Economic of Africa,* Ibadan: Longman.
Balandier, G. (1951): "The Colonial Situation: Theoretical Approach" in Immanuel Wallerstein (eds.) *Social Change: The Colonial Situation,* New York, John Wiley and Sons Inc.
Eaton, J. (1979) *Political Economy,* USA International Publishers.
Giddens, A. (1989) *Sociology: The Textbooks of the Nineties,* London: Polity Press.
Habermas, J. (1985) "Problems of Legitimation in Late Capitalism," in Cornaton, P. (ed) *Critical Sociology,* London: Penguin Books.
Hoogvelt, A. (1996) *Globalization and the Post-Colonial World: The New Political Economy of Development,* London: Macmillan.
Ikein, A. A. (1990) *The Impact of Oil in a Developing Country: The Case of Nigeria* Ibadan Evans (Nig.) Ltd.
Jelle, P. (1981) *The Pillage of the Third World,* New York: Monthly Review.
Lenin, V. I. (1979) *Imperialism: The Highest Stage of Capitalism,* Moscow: Progress Publishers.
Marx, K and Engels (1979) *Pre-capitalist Socio-economic Formations,* Moscow: Progress Publishers.
Miliband, R. (1979) *State in Capitalist Society,* USA Kegan Paul.
Nkrumah, K. (1965) *Neocolonialism: The Last Stage of Imperialism,* London Pana Books.
"Obasanjo has failed the Nation – verdict of the People on dividend of Democracy," in *Newswatch* Magazine, May 28, 2001.
Rodney, W. (1972) *How Europe Underdeveloped Africa,* Dar es Salam. Tanzania Book.
Warren, B. (1981) *Imperialism: Pioneer of Capitalism,* London, Verso.

5

The socio-cultural impact of globalization on Nigeria

– Suleiman B. Mohammed

Introduction

The decades of the 1990s and 2000s have been aptly described as the era of globalization in which the world has become a global village. This epoch has been marked by the dominance of capitalist values, institutions and system and phenomenal growth of information technology. This system is, however, divided into the developed and the developing world with contrasting socio-economic development, inequality and poverty. The advanced world has continued to develop in science, technology and socio-economic endeavours whilst the underdeveloped countries have remained stagnant and backward.

The historical evolution of globalization dates back to the emergence of capitalism and later imperialism. During the latter, several parts of the world were colonized and incorporated into the capitalist world economy at a peripheral level as suppliers of raw materials, market for manufactured goods and investment outlets. The process of globalization that started in the era was challenged by the emergence of socialism as an alternative socio-economic model in USSR and China. The demise of Soviet Union and the decline of socialism paved way for the consolidation of international capitalism through several economic (IMF, World Bank and WTO), political (UN), and military (NATO) agencies.

The emergence of global economy modelled after western capitalist system, values and principles has become a matter of celebration by bourgeois leaders and scholars. Where do Nigeria and other third world countries fit into this globalized world and what is the impact of the process on socio-cultural life of the people?

Conceptual and theoretical framework

Different scholars have described globalization variously. The concept connotes both a process and a situation of internalization of values, institution and system, a situation where values become global. It could also denotes universal civilization or westernization. Some scholars regard globalization as an indication of element of power relations between the advanced countries of the world and the Third World. In its ideological application, globalization is often seen as the universalization of western values, institutions and system over the traditional values of third world societies.

Globalization is economic, political and social in character. In economic terms, it is seen as increasing integration of national economies with the rest of the world its main features are:

> ...trace and capital flows (investment); increasing adoption of common or similar policies that govern economic relations between sovereign nations: creation and nurturing of institutions that support the process of integration in addition to integration in other areas such as national values, cultural beliefs as well as religious beliefs... (Shonekan, 2001:4).

Globalization ensures accessibility to markets and economies of scale facilitated through multilateral institutions such as World Bank, IMF and World Trade Organization (WTO) including the establishment of regional blocs. The power of information technology (IT) has also fostered globalization. Satellite broadcasting and computer technologies have transformed the world into a global village.

Globalization is also used inter-changeably with universal civilization or westernization. The issue of universal civilization implies the cultural union of humanity and the recognition of common values, orientation, practice and institutions by all the people of the world. This civilization is characterized by sheer belief in individualism, market economies, political democracy. The sources of universal civilization has been traced to the colonization of the third world and the extension of western political and economic domination, the decline of socialism and the collapse of USSR which ushered in a unipolar order. There is also the increasing interaction among peoples of the world facilitated by information technology in the areas of trade, investment, business etc. Universal civilization is also a product of modernization in the forms of industrialization, urbanization, increasing levels of literacy, education, wealth, social mobilization and complex occupational structures (Huntington, 1997).

The varied literature on globalization has been categorised into three clusters (i) "globalization as implying global culture and civilization" (ii) "globalization as referring to the global economy" the international division of labour, the new information technology revolution, and global capitalism or in the words of Wallerstein (1972), the modern world capitalist system is characterized by core, semi-periphery and peripheral states (actors) and (iii) "globalization is the expression of the global political and military orders (Abubakar, 2001:16).

In this chapter, globalization is taken to mean global culture and civilization imposed on the third world by the advanced countries in terms of the universalization of capitalist system, institutions and values. The work is based on the theoretical insight of V. I. Lenin on imperialism as the highest stage of capitalism and dependency theory articulated by Candoso, 1979 and Amin 1970, 1974).

The historical development of globalization could be traced to the development of imperialism, which was a specific stage in the development of capitalism as well as a form of relationship between two economics. V. I. Lenin characterized imperialism by five elements (i) the dominance of monopolies (ii) the dominance of finance capital (iii) the export of capital (iv) the formation of International monopolies (v) the petition of the world between the various imperialist powers (1978:21).

The export of capital and the colonization of the third world created a system of unequal exchange between the colonies of Africa, Asia and Latin America and the metropolitan centres of Europe and America. The former were producers of raw materials, providers of markets and places of investment while the latter provided manufactured goods and finance capital (Amin, 1974, 1976; Wallerstein 1972). Unequal exchange led to the development of dependency relationship where third world have their economies conditioned by the growth and expansion of another economy (Dos Santos 1970). A world capitalist system was created with centres in Europe and America and peripheral nations in Africa, Asia and Latin America. Wallerstein (1972) noted that the world capitalist system was divided into three centres: the core, the semi-periphery and the periphery. The emergence of socialism in Soviet Union in 1917 and China 1949 provided a challenge and alternative to the capitalist order. Consequently, a bipolar world structure was created. However, the demise of Soviet Union and the decline of socialism changed the global structure to unipolarism, hence, the celebration of globalization.

Globalization and socio-cultural life

Globalization has foisted on Nigeria a social system and values that are not only foreign but antithetical to socio-economic development of the country. The origin of the system dates back to the colonization of Nigeria in the nineteenth century by Britain. Hitherto, there were different societies with empires, kingdoms and chiefdoms that occupied the geo-political entity called Nigeria at different levels of socio-economic development. The prominent ones included Sokoto caliphate, Borno kingdom, Benin kingdom, Oyo empire, Igbo republics, etc. These were brought together under colonial domination in which capitalist relations were imposed. Colonial administration, taxation and currencies were introduced to those pre-capitalist societies (Ake 1980, William 1961, Onimode 1985, Akubo 1985). Consequently, capitalist relations were nurtured in Nigeria and the country became fully integrated into the world capitalist system as a supplier of raw materials (cocoa, groundnut, cotton, palm oil etc), markets for manufactured goods and areas of investment for TNCs.

Colonial economy incorporated Nigeria into international capitalists system through the colonial state, TNCs, marketing boards and monopoly over finance capital. Other mechanisms included control of public investment funds, tariffs, industrial and fiscal policies (Abba *et al* 1985, Williams 1981).

Thus at independence, Nigeria like most African countries, inherited a dependent economy which to a large extent was not serving the interests of Nigerians. The country was characterized by:

> ...puppet government represented by stooges and based on some chiefs, reactionary elements, anti-popular politicians, by bourgeois comprador and corrupted civil and military functionaries... independence after recognition of national sovereignty (The third All African Peoples Conference, Cairo 1961).

The foreign subordination and control of the economy has been strengthened through adjustment policies and clearance of annual budgets by creditor clubs (IMF and World Bank), monitoring units to assess progress and a permanent world banks representative in Nigeria to oversee the execution of austerity package (Akubo, 1985). The domination of Nigerian economy created two major classes, the dominant and the dominated. The former comprised of foreign bourgeois represented by managers of TNCs and the Nigerian petty bourgeoisie consisting of middlemen, professionals, doctors, lawyers, senior civil servants, top armed forces personnel. The dominated classes included labourers in public and private sectors, and large number of peasants, rural tenets farmers and lumpen elements. Imperialism has dominated Nigeria through collaboration of the dominant classes.

Given this political economy, politics became a game of "wheeling and dealing" (Williams 1981:55). It has been means of maintaining the status-quo of neo-colonialism and the privileges of the ruling elites. State power has become so critical for the survival of neo-colonial order has a means of primitive accumulation using the allocative and distributive power of the state. The struggle for the sharing of the national cake has been very central to the struggle to acquire power in Nigeria. Politics has since independence become a "zero-sum game" in which opposition is ruthlessly suppressed. The militarization of politics since 1960s was essentially to resolve neo-colonial contradiction as well as intra-bourgeois squabbles for hegemony.

Neo-colonial political economy in Nigeria has generated monumental socio-economic and political crisis in the forms of raging economic crisis, poverty, political instability, ethno-religious conflicts, etc. The state has been able to manage some of these contradictions. The enormous wealth generated in Nigeria largely through agriculture and oil has been plundered by TNCs and Nigeria elites through corruption and prebendalism. Consequently, majority of Nigerians are living in absolute poverty.

Globalization for Nigeria means the deepening of neo-colonial dependency in the forms of foreign investment through TNCs, loans, grants and aid from IMF, World Bank and clubs of finance capital in London, Paris and New York. It also meant political integration through the agencies of united nation and common wealth. At the political level, it also entails political democracy as an acceptable bourgeois form of governance. At the social level, increased access to information through information technology. How have these changes in the structure of dependency impacted on the socio-cultural life of Nigerians? This will be examined in the areas of value system, social system and institutions and education and knowledge.

Value system

Globalization has imposed on Nigeria, the capitalist value system in the name of universal civilization. These values include some beliefs in individualism, market principle and political democracy. The principle of individualism was enunciated in the era of the rise of capitalism in its struggle against feudal absolutism. It upholds that the individual is endowed with certain capabilities and rights by nature, which ought to be respected. These include freedom and right to life, property, association, justice, liberty etc. In practice, the principle acknowledges the right of individuals to work and acquire property, enjoy legal and political freedom and social status.

These contradict the pre-capitalist African principle of collectivism and brotherhood common among Nigerian people. Family members and the community at large anchored Nyerere's popular thesis of African socialism on African communal values where land, tools and property were shared. In Nigeria, several ethnic groups collectively cultivated the land and shared the product. However, the principle of collectivism and brotherhood has been eroded and in its place individualism has taken over, especially among the elites in urban centres. This has created many vices such as corruption, mismanagement and all sorts of fraud in a bid to achieve personal wealth. Related to this example is the over glorification of wealth where individuals are at pressure to acquire wealth at all cost and by all means in contemporary Nigeria.

The market economy here refers to the capitalist system, which is based on the centrality of the market. The institution of the market is used as a means of allocating resources as well as fixing prices of goods and services. It assumes the existence of "invisible forces", particularly those of demand and supplies that work automatically to regulate the economy. Market economy principles provide a diminishing role of the state in economic matters that is restricted to provision of enabling atmosphere for economic endeavours. The popularity and propagation of this principle was intensified with the collapse of Soviet Union and the decline of socialism.

This was seen as a triumph for capitalism as the only viable economic system in the world. In Nigeria, there has been an aggressive emphasis on market as a value system. Successive Nigerian governments have concerned themselves with the provisions of enabling atmosphere for foreign investment and security for TNCs, especially those involved in oil business in the southern part of the country. These regimes have embarked on privatization and commercialization as way of reverting to complete market principle. The programme of privatization and commercialization was started in 1986 as an integral component of SAP policy. Various arguments bordering on revival, efficiency and effectiveness have been put forward to justify the programme of privatization in Nigeria. The globalization context of the Nigerian political economy has made privatization an attractive policy option for now.

Political democracy entails the existence of political plurality akin to the market where citizens have options to choose among competing interests. Globalization has anti-authoritarian disposition including military dictatorship. Many third world autocratic regimes have been compelled to surrender power to the democratic process. Nigeria has benefited from this principle when the leading capitalist nations and agencies imposed limited sanctions on Nigeria military juntas because of their failure to hand over power to civilian in 1996. The pressures mounted by the USA, Britain, Canada and France as well as the IMF and World Bank contributed to the collapse of authoritarian regimes in third world, including Nigeria. The issuance of loan, aid and grants were all tied to good human rights and democratic credentials. Globalization has anti-military and authoritarian disposition as a means of protecting the constitutive interests of the elites.

However, liberal democracy has serious limitations in terms of providing rights and privileges to citizens, especially the poor people. Liberalism emphasized more on legal and political rights, which in most third world are observed more in breach than practice. Liberal democracy is unable to empower people because it does not provide economic empowerment. In most liberal democracies including those in USA and Britain, the electoral choice is between the same interest with only slight differences in approach and strategy. The poor are marginalized and alienated and therefore democracy does not make much sense to them. The Nigerian experience has failed to produce sufficient "dividend" for the masses. Political openings have been used to unleash ethno-religious conflicts. Corruption has continued unabated whilst the people have remained impoverished. Political democracy can only be relevant if it is used to push for a popular democracy and the transformation of market economy to people oriented economy. Political democracy in the forms of multi-partyism, rule of law, constitutionalism does not in themselves translate to participation. Allen *et al.* (1992:10) points that:

> Multi-partyism and the rule of law, indeed even the codification of basic human rights, do not of themselves employ participation, representativeness, accountability or transparency. They may be essential to the possibility of reducing inequalities and of removing oppression, but do not accomplish those of their own accord. Much more commonly democracy serves as a system through which class dominance and various form of systematic inequalities are perpetuated and legitimated. The challenge of those African nations undergoing a process of democratization is to use space it opens to press for greater justice for the mass of the population.

System and institutions

Globalization has impacted negatively on the social system and institution nurtured over the period of colonialism and neo-colonialism in Nigeria. The dependent capitalist socio-economic system inherited after independence, which has been based on import of manufactured goods and export of raw materials has been made to see itself as part of a world-wide market. The market appears to down play the role of the state and emphasized the capacity of individuals as entrepreneurs. Globalization has also perfected the IMF, World Bank, WTO and finance clubs as veritable instruments of global economic interaction. The impression of a global economy that Nigeria is a part is misleading. Collins Leys (1996:17) made the point aptly:

> Our leaders are currently directing a process of self-destruction of our societies in the name of an utopia no less irrational than the beliefs of the solar temple... this utopia is the idea of a world wide market in which the people of the world relate to each other directly as individuals, and only as individuals, and globalization (linked in turn to acceptance of the unchecked freedom of capital to move across national boundaries) is a process of trying to realize this ideal.

The emphasis on globalization has diverted the attention of Nigerian masses from the critical issues of poverty in the midst of affluence/massive corruption, which has created a comprador bourgeoisie, etc. Concern has shifted to the provision of an enabling environment for foreign investment.

Globalization has foisted certain changes in the system and institutions of society. The institution of marriage and family has seen many changes in terms of mode of contracting marriages from traditional to church/mosque and court marriages. The symbols of marriages such as rings, dresses, cake, gown, perfumes have attained enormous modernization. The family has had to contain with changing functions in such areas like socialization. The concept of single parenthood has now become global with all its negative effect on the child and society.

The media and communication industry has also changed drastically. Information technology, Internet and e-mail have made the world a global village. We now have global movie, television and video industry. This has profound impact on the lives of the people of Nigeria. It has negatively affected the training and socialization process where children now watch amoral movie and try to copy it. Satellite broadcasting has also become a powerful ideological tool used by America and her allies to control the minds of people and change their attitudes.

Other areas include the promotion of pop culture and western consumer goods (car, TV sets, cameras, electronic gadgets, etc.) Our attitude on dressing has equally changed. It is a common fact now to see people dressed in jeans, listening to rap music. Globalization has also influenced Nigerians on matters like food such as fizzy liquids and fatty food, which is gradually replacing local delicacies.

The impact of globalization is manifest in the political institution of the country. Globalization has nurtured a brand of politics in third world including Nigeria that is different from true democracy. Politics is based on ethnic, religious and monetary considerations (Nnoli 1980, Usman 1987, Egwu 1990.) There is a 'winner-take-all' syndrome, prebendalism and corruption has pervaded the political environment. Electoral rigging and malpractices are widespread. The most negative political implication of globalization on politics is suppression of state and society under the disguise of universal civilization. Globalization's emphasis on freedom of capital flow across the globe contradicts the reality of state and society. Democracy under the present milieu is difficult to create, nurture and sustain. Manifred Bienefeld (1995:52) notes:

> Unfortunately genuine democracy is hard to reconcile with neo-liberalism's mystical belief in the magic of disembodied markets, its fierce hostility to the notion of state and society as organic entities capable of defining and pursuing a common interest, and its insistence on pervasive deregulation. Under such conditions, the State loses the capacity to manage economics in accordance with democratically determined social, ethical and political priorities. Only the shallowest and most meaningless democracy will survive a "cowboy capitalism" where property rights become virtually absolute because states and electorates are disempowered by the mobility of capital.

Education and knowledge

Colonialism through missionaries introduced western education in Africa, including Nigeria to facilitate evangelisation. Much later the colonial state became involved in education to train middle-level manpower. Colonial education was biased against science education. This trend continued in the post-colonial Nigeria with more emphasis on arts, social sciences and teacher education. A critical issue on education is the brain drain to America and Europe where there are better incentives and facilities. Scholarship and knowledge in most third world project western societies as model for the developing countries to copy and deliberately distort and misrepresent the social reality of Africa. Claude Ake (1979: viii) succinctly noted:

> Western social sciences scholarship on developing countries amounts to imperialism...in the sense that (a) it foists or at any rate attempt to foist on the developing countries, capitalist values, capitalist institutions and capitalists development (b) it focuses social science analysis on the question of how to make the developing countries more like the west and it propagates mystification, and modes of thought and action which serve the interests of imperialism.

The essence of western social sciences, which is peddled in Africa as objective scholarship, is to maintain the system of neo-colonialism. This system has retained the economic dependence of Africa on the west in spite of formal independence. The major problem of this form of knowledge is its Eurocentric character. There is also the tendency to equate ideal situations with the reality. Western systems of socio-economic and political forms are projected as ideal models for Africa to copy. Western system, institutions and values were seen as model for Africa to adopt in their process of modernization. Eurocentric scholarship has reinforced the system of socio-economic dependency created and sustained during and after colonialism. It creates inferiority complex among the Africans in relationship to the Europeans. Western social sciences scholarship does not recognize the fundamental needs for radical transformation of the socio-economic and political system in Africa.

Globalization has sustained this reactionary conception of knowledge in Africa. It has also encouraged the massive brain drain taking place in Africa and as such constitutes an impediment to the development of Africa. The IMF and World Bank in collaboration with Nigerian ruling classes are also determined to deny access to education for majority of qualified candidates. The Nigeria University System Innovation Project (NUSIP) embarked upon by the Government in collaboration with World Bank and IMF illustrates the negative attitude of the ruling elites to the issues of accessibility and quality in Nigerian education. The programme in principle is designed to revitalize the Nigerian university system through the infusion of one hundred million dollar loan. However, it is a clear ploy designed to subjugate and control the Nigerian university system by forces of imperialism. It will raise cost of education and deny accessibility to poor students. It can be discerned that globalization have impacted negatively on the socio-economic transformation of Nigeria. A system of dependency, unequal exchange and underdevelopment has been fostered by globalization.

Conclusion

Globalization imposed a dependent capitalist social system and western values in the forms of individualism, market principle and institutions on Nigeria. The traditional life style of the people has been relegated to the background as primitive while European lifestyles tagged modern is being foisted. A culture of dependency also was institutionalized through the internationalization of capital and social life. Nigeria traditional values and principles on marriage and family, education, norms and values are all being eroded.

Underdevelopment and inferiority complex were also instituted as a cumulative product of western hegemony on Nigerians. The sorry condition of life in economic, political, educational and cultural fields would in part be attributed to globalization. For Nigeria to be an effective actor in the global community certain fundamental and critical changes must be done to the state and society. The state must be done to the state and society. The state must be reconstituted to take into cognizance the interest of majority of Nigerians and provide an enabling environment for creativity and productivity. The structures of neo-colonialism embodied in the state must be destroyed in order to make the state responsive to the yearnings of the people for socio-economic and technological development without dictate from imperialism.

The value system of the Nigerian society must be transformed from being capitalist in nature, which emphasized individualism, market principle, dependency and political democracy to a self reliant and people-centred socio-economic development. Nigerians must be mobilized and educated to understand and appreciate the smokescreen behind the slogan of globalization. At the same time, a selfless leadership committed to the revival of the value of African brotherhood and community spirit is required for the eventual emancipation of Nigeria from neo-imperialism (globalization).

References

Abba, A. *et al* (1985) *Nigerian Economic Crisis: Causes and Solutions*, Zaria: Gaskiya Publishers.

Abubakar, D. (2001) "Globalization, Social Sciences and Nigeria in the 21st Century," *Newsletters of SSAN,* Vol. 4, No. 16, pp. 15-19.

Allen, C. *et al* (1992) "Surviving Democracy?" *Review of Africa Political Economy*, 54 (3).

Akubo, O. (1985) *Medical Professionalism and State Power,* Jos: Ehindero Press.

Amin, S. (1974) *Accumulation on a World Scale*, New York: Monthly Review Press.

Amin, S. (1976) *Unequal Development: An Essay in the Social Formation of Peripheral State*, New York: Monthly Review Press.

Bienefeld, F. H. and Paletto, E (1979) *Dependency and Development in Latin America,* Berkeley, University of California.

Giddens, A. (1998) *Sociology: the Textbook of the Nineties*, UK: Polity Press.

Huntington, S. (1974) *Clash of Civilisation*, London: Macmillan.

Lenin, V. I. (1978) *Imperialism: The Highest Stage of Capitalism*, Moscow: Progress Publishers.

Leys, C. (1994) "Confronting the African Tragedy," *New Left Review* 254 (March - April).

Magdoff, H. (1969) *The Age of Imperialism: The Economics of US Foreign Policy*, New York: Monthly Review Press.

Nkrumah, K. (1945) *Neo-colonialism: The Last Stage of Imperialism*, London: Panaf.

Nnoli, O. (1978) *Ethnic Politics in Nigeria*, Enugu: Fourth Dimension Publishers.

Nyerere, J. (1969) *Freedom and Unity*, East Africa, Oxford University Press.

Offiong, D. (1980) *Imperialism and Dependency*, Enugu: Fourth Dimension.

Onimode, B (1985) *An introduction to Marxist Political Economy,* London, ZED.

Peter, S., "Modernity: Sociological categories and identities," in *Current Sociology*, London vol. 48 (3) July 2001.

Rodney, W. (1982) *How Europe Underdeveloped Africa*, Enugu: Ikenga Publishers.

Saul, J.S. "'For fear of being condemned as old fashioned': Liberal Democracy vs Popular Democracy in sub-Saharan Africa", *Review of African Political Economy* (ROAPFC) vol. 24, p.339.

Shonekan, E. A., "The Challenges of Globalization and Privatisation in Nigeria," Conference on Consolidating Democracy in Nigeria, Yakubu Gowon Centre, Abuja, July 4-7, 2000.

Toyo, E. (2001) "Background to Globalization," in *Delusions of a Popular Paradigm: Essays on Alternative Path to Economic Development*, Nigerian Economic Society.

Usman, Y. B. (1987) *Manipulation of Religion in Nigeria*, Kaduna: Vanguard Press.

Williams, H. (1981) *State and Society in Nigeria*, Idanre: Afrografice.

Wallerstein I. (1972) *Unequal Exchange: A Study of Imperialism of Trade*, New York, Monthly Review Press.

6

An analysis of import revenue in Nigeria within the context of globalized trade policy

– Chika Umar Aliyu

Introduction

Nigeria is bestowed with abundant human and material resources such as petroleum, gold limestone, etc. The country also is blessed with vast arable land estimated as 923,773 square kilometres with different vegetational zones suitable for agricultural and other activities. The population was estimated in 1995 at 111.7 million. It has also been projected that given the annual population growth rate of 3%, the population has tendency to rise up to 163 million people by the year 2015 CE.[1]

The economy is agrarian in nature with agriculture serving as the mainstay of the economy considering its contribution to GDP. The main objectives of the agricultural sector are (i) food supply, (ii) provision of employment, (iii) poverty alleviation, (v) supply of raw materials to industry and (v) diversification of the economy. The manufacturing sector is also another major contributor to GDP. Some of the goods produced by the manufacturing sector are petroleum products and other assembly type consumer goods e.g. Peugeot cars. The most salient objectives of manufacturing sector are (i) enhanced contribution to GDP (ii) addition to foreign exchange and government revenues, and (iii) poverty alleviation.

As far as Nigerian industrial/trade policies are concerned, they were designed towards import-substitution. The policy of import substituting imported goods with locally produced items. Thus, machinery and equipment are to a large extent raw materials were to be imported while cash crops and

---

[1] Refer to Nigeria (1985), "The Effects of Population on Social and Economic Development," prepared under the direction of Federal Ministry Health and National Population Bureau, p.5.

crude oil would continue to be exposed (Aliyu, 1998). To intensify the policy of import substitution, government embarked on investment on heavy industries like steel, fertilizers, etc. and financial institutions such as development banks, insurance companies, etc. The policy recorded little success due to the huge cost of projects and mismanagement of public investments, which resulted into abandoned/white elephant projects (Aliyu, 1998).

In 1972, Nigeria came up with indigenization policy so as to reduce the dominance of multi-national corporations in private sector economic pursuits in areas such as banking, retail trading, oil, etc. This recorded little success because the ownership of targeted business did not necessarily transfer to Nigerians, foreign direct investment reduced and foreign investors left the nation. Seeing this adverse effect, trade liberalization policy was embarked upon in 1986 as a product of structural adjustment programme (SAP) recommended by IMF in order to reduce protection and liberalise imports (Bankole and Olayiwola, 2000; Aliyu, 1988). In 1994, Guided Deregulation Economic Reforms (GDER) was introduced in the course of implementing SAP. With guided deregulation, the government restricted itself to providing environment for investments and supervisory roles allowing market forces to decide prevailing economic parameters import revenue in Nigeria and finally section five presents summary conclusion and recommendation.

Theoretical framework

The theoretical framework upon which analysis in this chapter is based is drawn from Richardian static theory of relative comparative advantage. The theory of comparative advantage suggests that nations should produce and export goods for which they have relative comparative advantage over other countries given their factor endowment; and import those goods for which they have no comparative advantage in the midst of other nations. Later other postulations emerged such as Heckscher–Ohlin Learner–Samuelson (HOLS) models known as neo-classical models all suggesting the same thing except the little dynamism and sophistication they have above Richardian Static Model (see Evans 1981, Scemogereie and Kasekende, 1994).

As part of the theoretical construct, we shall also depict graphical illustrations of free-trade equilibrium formulated by Caves and Jones (1977).

The choice of Richardian and neo-classical theories and graphical illustration of Caves and Jones (1977) is purposive because they lean towards internationalization and integration of trade policies, which form the genesis of the concept globalization though it is a recent concept. The relevant illustration is depicted and explained below.

Figure 1: Caves and Jones graphical illustration of free trade equilibrium

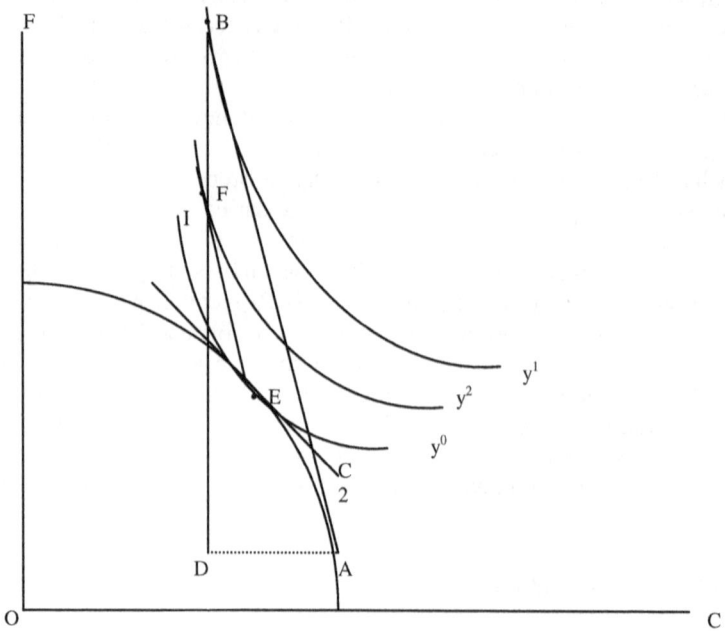

In the above figure, the free-trade prices are shown by the slope of line 2, production at home takes place at A and consumption at H. EDA is the trade-triangle - the community exports DA units of clothing in exchange for imports of BD units of food. The figure exhibits the outcome of trade and its implication for home country. Assuming this country is not allowed to engage in international trade, its consumption possibilities are limited to points on TT' curve of which the best is point E where indifference curve Yo is tangent to TT'. The free-trade relative price of clothing, which clears he market, is shown by slope of line 1. But with opening of trade via globalization, world prices are shown by the slope of line 2. Thus, the benefits from trade are shown but the increase in real income denoted by movement from curve of y_0 to this higher curve i.e. yi. Caves and Jones, (1977) concluded that in a free-trade equilibrium the home-country's import demand for food (etc) must be matched by the foreign country's willingness to export it. This apparently refers to the case of globalization as we come to know it nowadays.

Review of literature

Having specified the theoretical framework for this study, it is imperative now examine the relevant literature. This section will review the debate between free trade and protectionism and also the concept of globalization.

(a) Free-trade versus protectionism

As observed by Olurunshola (1996), the role of trade in the growth process has been inadequately explored in the literature. But still despite the gains from international trade some writers prefer protectionism. This difference was highlighted as follows:

> With and between countries there are often schools of thoughts among economists as well as, and indeed, particularly between politicians about free trade or protectionism. The advocates of protectionism are not, in the process opposed to international trade; they are usually concerned with the protection of specific economic sectors which they consider to be of special, sometimes value to their own countries.[2]

Among the advocates of free trade, Evans (1981) argued in favour of free trade between countries and stressed that it is a matter of enormous importance to notice that due to the gains from international trade radicalists such as Marx had nothing to do but to side with Ricardo on free trade. Thirlwall (2000,a) opined that trade liberalization promotes economic growth though improving efficiency and stimulating exports which have powerful effects on both supply and demand within the economy.

Flanders (1981) in response to this observed that protection in the periphery cannot be expected to cause significant reduction in the prices of its import because the centre's biggest customer is itself not the periphery. We can understand here that Flanders did not see protectionism as the solution. Olurunshola (1981) replied to the advocates of protectionism in favour of infant industries that high protective tariffs could even reduce government revenue because they choke off imports of manufactured goods. This means that where imports are not allowed in the home country, government is denied revenue through custom duties, etc. He further added that protection that protectionist measures tend to sustain inefficient industries at the expense of more efficient ones and render the protected industries perpetual infants![3]

Looking towards protectionism, Prebish (1959) advocate for protectionism because according to him peripheral countries have experienced long-run deterioration in their terms of trade with the centre and that they should counteract this by imposing tariffs on industrial imports. Kindleberger as [cited by Yesufu 1986] supported protectionism arguing on the basis of terms of trade. According to him there is tendency that the term of trade may worsen for developing countries and favour developed nations if free trade is allowed without protection. Like others who support protectionism due to terms of trade argument, Ellsworth (1981) also opined that peripheral countries need to adopt protectionism because:

> The prices of primary products rise more rapidly than industrial prices in the upswing, but also they fall more in the down swing, so that in the course of the cycles the gap between prices of the two is progressively widened. The reason for this is very simple. Owing to imperfect competition among industrial producers and to the supervisor organization of labour in the centre countries, prices of industrial products and wages of industrial workers are relatively rigid during the downswing.

(b) Globalization

The concept of globalization is gaining momentum and becoming increasingly popular. Following the end of ideological polarization of the world observed by Obaseki (1991), the trend in globalization has been sustained by the rapid liberalization of trade and capital flows between nations. This is obvious because with the collapse of former Soviet Union and the end of the Cold War, strict protection disappeared and nations became more open.

One would like to know the definition and meaning of this concept that is becoming realistic every now and then. Kwanashie (1999:18) maintained that *"Globalization can also be defined as the process of shifting autonomous economies into a global system of production and distribution."* Kwanashie further added that distribution is a process-increased integration of national economies with the rest of the world to create a more coherent global economy.

According to CBN Annual Report (1997:18 1), Globalization *"is the rapid integration of productive and investment decisions across the world by economic agents desirous of taking advantages of the environments where their competitive edge can manifest in high returns."*

Like any other thing, globalization requires some enabling environment so that its full benefits can be realized. Philips (1999) buttress that democratization, economic growth, effective banking system, well organized and developed profit – motivated private sector, discipline citizenry, liberalization, etc., will ensure maximum benefits from globalization. Therefore, any nation that lacks these issues is unlikely to fit well in the globalization.

The CBN Annual Report of 1997 highlighted on some of the benefits of globalization as follows:

> *under a globalized setting consumers buy more foreign goods, firms operate across national borders and savers invest more abroad thereby increasing the potential to*

*boost productivity and living standards of the countries The same Report also
further pointed at the benefits of globalization such as increase in specialization
and efficiency better quality products at reduced prices, consumer satisfaction, etc.*
(emphasis mine)

Profile of import values and revenues

Liberalization was pursued with the aim of achieving both internal and external
balances, which previous controls and restrictions could not achieve. For
liberalization to be effective import licensing was abolished together with
commodity boards. The abolition of commodity boards enabled exporters to
market their products directly without any hindrance (CBN, 2000). At the end of
1995 the federal government reduced the list of banned imports to 1.3 items and
only 4 export items were banned.

In addition to trade policy of liberalization Nigeria also adopted Tariff
Regimes over the years with a view of improve trade balance and increase
revenue. In 1995 Customs and Excise Tariffs Decree No. 4 was introduced to
replace 1988–1994 tariff regime. The new tariff regime aimed at among
lowering other things protection rate, reducing the import and export prohibition
lists, cutting down customs and excise duties, etc. In general, the new tariff
regime of 1995 further liberalized the country's international trade transactions
(CBN, 2000).

In this chapter our assertion is that globalization will enable more contact
with outside world and hence ensures more import revenues via trade
liberalization. With this assertion posited, the chapter proceeds to present review
of literature and theoretical frame work in sections two and three respectively,
section four attempts to provide information and data on import values/revenues
to see whether our assertion is true to untrue as the case may be.

Nigeria has revealed comparative advantage for certain manufactured goods,
which can be exported to other nations. Similarly those goods for which the
country has no comparative advantage can be imported from other countries; but
all these depend on existence of liberalized trade policy, which is part and parcel
of globalization. The benefit, which Nigeria stands to get if importation is
allowed, is in two folds. First, the tariffs and custom duties charged on imports
constitute some revenues to the government, which could not be obtained if no
importation is allowed at all. Second, through importation people can have
access to goods and services they need that improve their living standard. In this
chapter we shall restrict ourselves to only the import revenues.

Appendix II shows the Nigeria's foreign trade in agriculture commodities.
Exports and imports are show for the period of about three decades (i.e. 1970 –
1999). Looking at the trend in import we can see that food imports grew from
₦57.7 million to ₦1473.5 million in 1950 and rose to ₦1761.1 million in 1983.

This development of growth in import was the case despite the import substitution policies embarked by the government. This inflow of imports was accompanied by tariff rates, which constituted revenue to the government. The trend in export from 1970 to 1983 was declining which indicated a negative terms of trade for the agricultural sector. Therefore, though absolute liberalization policy was not by them embarked on, yet terms of trade worsened falsifying claims of advocates of protectionism.

Still from Appendix II we can observe that in response to structural adjustment programme (SAP) policies, agricultural production improved from 1986 to 1999. The reason for this markedly rises in production (export) and import is largely due to liberalization policy, which is an ingredient of concept of globalization. Looking at volume of imports more generally, we will also notice the sharp increase immediately after the introduction of SAP in 1986 which is a bye-product of liberalization policy as shown below. Table 1 shows that from 1986 when naira value of import was ₦5,947m, it rose to ₦165,629.4m in 1993. It is also the same story if we look at the value in US Dollar, because in 1986 value of import was $3449.0m, which rose to $6625.2m in 1993. As earlier stated imports generates substantial revenue to the nation through the tariffs, import duties. The table below shows import duties, government revenues and taxes on international trade and transactions from 1980–1994.

Table 1: Value of imports in Nigeria (₦m) and US Dollar

Year	Imports Naira (Nm)	Dollar (Sm)
1982	10,100.1	15,0005.3
1983	6,555.7	38,733.7
1984	4,484.5	5,845.3
1985	5,536.9	6,201.0
1986	5,974.7	3,449.0
1987	15,698.1	3,995.1
1988	17,645.1	3,889.4
1989	25,175.3	3,418.2
1990	34,704.7	4,317.7
1991	53,496.1	5,396.6
1992	122,426.1	6,195.9
1993	165,629.4	6,625.2

Source: Adapted from Yesufu (1996: 303)

Table 2: Import duties, government revenue and taxes on international trade and transactions

Year	Import duties	Government revenue	Taxes on international trade and transactions
1980	-	-	
1985	11.5	12.4	11.7
1986	16.2	17.2	16.4
1987	NA	16.0	NA
1988	NA	17.3	NA
1989	NA	15.6	NA
1990	NA	20.7	NA
1991	NA	21.2	NA
1992	NA	17.6	NA
1993	NA	115.4	NA
1994	NA	10.5	NA
Annual average			
1995-84	16.1	17.5	16.1
1985-89	11.4	14.5	11.6
1990-	NA	17.1	NA

Source: African Development Indicators, pp 187, 191 & 192
* The figures exclude grants. NA= Not Available

From table 2 above the import duties comprise all levies collected on goods imported into the country excluding consumption or commodity taxes levied on domestic goods. The figures shown under the column of import duties are percentages of total revenue. The figures under the column of government revenue are percentages of GPD in naira value. The figures under the column of taxes on international trade and transactions show percentages of total revenue and they include among other things both import and export duties. Looking at the trend of these indicators one sees clearly that it is not encouraging and much is desired. This discouraging value of revenue is not unconnected with the slowness of the nation to be active participant in globalization process. The nation has high prospects of getting much import revenue if it actively participates in the globalization process looking at the customs duty rate for some selected items as shown by appendix III.

Summary, conclusion and recommendations

This highlighted on the Nigerian economy by explaining the trade policies of the country at different phases. The chapter also offered model of international trade. Graphics illustration of free trade was also adopted for Caves and Jones (1997) in order to serve as the basis of this chapter. A review of related literature was also done. The chapter also attempted to look at profile of import values and revenue. At this juncture we can conclude that Nigeria has much prospect to benefit from its involvement in foreign trade if it gives way to globalization process. We can see this clearly from the fact that the liberalization policy embarked upon in 1986 when SAP was introduced led to positive changes in most indicators. Therefore, for Nigeria to continue reaping gains from foreign trade and realize steady economic growth, we offer the following recommendations:

(i)   Inefficient public enterprises should be privatized and commercialized to make the economy market oriented.

(ii)   The economy should be opened and liberalized

(iii) The nation needs to be placed on real and sound democratic footing to obtain stable and peaceful government.

(iv)   There should be well-organised and effective financial system in the country to facilitate transactions.

(v)   There should be intensive efforts to fight corruption and restore discipline among the citizens so as to reassure the international community.

References

Africa Development Bank (1997) *Selected Statistic on Regional Member Countries*, ADB publication.

Aliyu, A. (1998) *Nigeria Economic Breakthrough: The Abacha Strategies*, FEAP, Abuja, Nigeria.

Bagwati, J. N. (1969) *Trade Tariff and Growth*, MIT, USA.

Bankole, A.S. and M. A. Olayiwola (2000) "Industrial Trade and Export Promotion Policies and Revealed Comparative Advantage of Nigeria Manufactured Exports," A Paper Presented at the Millennium Conference of the Nigerian Economic Society (NES), Held at Abuja between 27th August and 1st September.

Caves, R. E. and R.W. Jones, (1977) *World Trade and Payments: An Introduction*, 2nd ed., Little, Brown and Company, Toronto, Canada.

CBN (1997) *Annual Report and Statement of Accounts for the Year Ended 31st December*, Central Bank of Nigeria Publication, Abuja.

CBN (2000) *The Changing Structure of the Nigerian Economy and Implications for Development*, Central Bank Publication, Abuja, Nigeria.

Ellsworth, P.T. (1981) "The Terms of Trade Between Primary – Producing and Industrial Countries," in Livingstone, I. (ed.) *Development Economics and Policy: Readings*, George Allen and Unwin, London, pp. 129 – 136.

Flanders, N.J. (1981) "Prebisch On Protectionism: An Evaluation," in Livingstone, I. (ed.) *Development Economics and Policy: Readings*, pp. 108–166.

Kwanashie, M., (1999) "Concepts and Dimension of Globalization," in *Globalization and Nigeria's Economic Development*, proceeding of the One-day Seminar held at the

Nigeria Institute of International Affairs, Lagos, Nigeria Economic Society, Lagos, Nigeria.

Nigeria (1985) *The Effects of Population on Social and Economic Development*, prepared Under the Direction of Federal Ministry of Health and National Population Bureau.

Obaseki, P.J. (1999) "Policies and Strategies for Dealing with the Problems of Globalization," in *Globalization and Nigeria's Economic Development, op. cit*, pp. 65 – 87.

Okongwu C.S.P. (1986) *The Nigerian Economy: An Anatomy of a Traumatised Economy with Some Proposals for Stabilization*, Fourth Dimension, Enugu, Nigeria.

Olurunshola, J.A. (1996) "Export-Led Growth in Economic Development Lessons of Experience," *CBN Bullion*, Vol. 20, No. 4, October/December.

Philips, D. (1999) "Not a Chance," in *Globalization and Nigeria's Economic Development*, pp. 9–14.

Prebisch, R. (1959) "International Payments in an Era of Co-existence: Commercial Policy in the Underdeveloped Countries," *American Economic Review*, Vol. 49, No. 2, pp. 251 –273.

Ricardo, D. (1817) *Principles of Political Economy and Taxation*, London, Everyman, (1992)

Ssemogerere, G.N. and L.A. Kasekende, (1994) *Constraints to the Development and Diversification of Non-Traditional Exports in Uganda 1981-90*, AERC Research Papers, No. 28.

Thirlwill, A. P. (2000a) *Trade Liberalization and Economic Growth: Theory and Evidence*, Economic Research Papers, No. 63, A.D.B. Abidjan, Cote d'Ivore

Thirlwill, A. P. (2000a) "Trade Agreements, Trade Liberalization and Economic Growth: A Selective Study," *African Development Review*, Vol. 12 No.2 December, pp. 129-160.

Usman, S. (1999) "Implications of Globalization for the Nigerian Economy," in *Globalization and Nigeria's Economic Development, op. cit.*, pp. 45 – 63.

World Bank (1995) *Globalization, Economic Prospects and the Developing Countries*, Washington DC, USA.

Yesufu, T. M. (1996) *The Nigerian Economy: Growth Without Development*, Benin Social Science Series for Africa, University of Benin, Benin City, Nigeria.

Appendix I: Balassa index of revealed comparative advantage for Nigeria's manufacturers

Year	Food, Beverages and Tobacco	Crude materials	Animals and vegetable oils	Mineral fuels and related materials	Chemicals	Machinery and transport equipment	Other manufactured goods
1970	1.375	1.594	4.492	5.975	0.004	0.000	0.162
1971	0.970	0.901	2.257	6.865	0.006	0.000	0.041
1972	0.669	0.577	1.60 1	6.784	0.006	0.000	0.087
1973	0.545	0.755	2.022	6.041	0.005	0.000	0.074
1974	0.271	0.312	0.890	5.990	0.003	0.000	0.030
1975	0.364	0.184	0.404	4.770	0.003	0.000	0.035
1976	0.338	0.119	0.095	4.627	0.002	0.000	0.032
1977	0.450	0.123	0.083	4.653	0.003	0.000	0.034
1978	0.616	0.136	0.279	5.176	0.001	0.000	0.067
1979	0.275	0.127	0.279	4.608	0.002	0.000	0.027
1980	0.148	0.058	0.195	3.720	0.009	0.000	0.021
1981	0.188	0.058	0.122	3.947	0.004	0.000	0.024
1982	0.192	0.050	0.059	4.079	0.000	0.000	0.025
1983	0.341	0.053	0.105	4.342	0.000	0.000	0.079
1984	0.258	0.033	0.103	4.691	0.001	0.000	0.088
1985	0.221	0.021	0.007	5.056	0.001	0.000	0.041
1986	0.496	0.107	0.025	7.305	0.002	0.000	0.048
1987	0.318	0.131	0.016	8.168	0.025	0.000	0.026
1988	0.680	0.195	0.056	9.312	0.071	0.004	0.068
1989	0.231	0.513	0.000	9.362	0.044	0.003	0.034
1990	0.191	0.151	0.000	9.274	0.023	0.003	0.031
1991	0.178	0.148	0.000	8.548	0.034	0.004	0.026
1992	0.171	0.154	0.000	8.908	0.033	0.003	0.021
1993	0.246	0.78	0.000	8.941	0.044	0.004	0.03 1
1994	0.235	0.150	0.000	8.958	0.044	0.004	0.03 1
1995	0.224	0.126	0.000	8.973	0.044	0.005	0.031
1996	0.214	0.106	0.000	8.985	0.044	0.005	0.032
Average 1970-74	0.766	0.828	2.253	6.331	0.005	0.000	0.092
Average 75-80	0.365	0.124	0.222	4.593	0.003	0.000	0.036
Average 70-85	0.451	0.3 19	0.812	5.083	0.003	0.000	0.058
Average 1986-96	0.297	0.185	0.012	8.775	0.036	0.003	0.035

Source: Bankole and Olayiwola, (2000:15)

Appendix II: Nigeria's foreign trade in agricultural commodities (₦ million)

Year	Exports	% Share of agriculture in total export	Food imports	Share of food in total import %
1970	265.2	30.0	57.7	7.6
1971	242.8	18.8	88.3	8.2
1972	164.8	11.6	95.8	9.7
1973	250.1	10.9	126.3	10.3
1974	276.0	4.7	154.8	8.9
1975	230.6	4.7	298.8	8.0
1976	274.1	4.1	441.7	8.6
1977	375.7	4.9	780.7	11.0
1978	412.8	6.8	1027.6	12.5
1979	468.0	4.8	1254.3	16.8
1980	340.1	2.4	1437.5	15.8
1981	113.2	1.0	1819.6	14.2
1982	198.6	2.4	1642.3	15.2
1983	431.2	5.8	1761.1	19.8
1984	288.8	3.2	1349.7	18.8
1985	192.1	1.6	1199.0	17.0
1986	407.4	4.6	801.9	13.4
1987	937.4	3.1	1873.8	10.5
1988	1780.4	5.7	1891.6	8.8
1989	1726.8	3.0	2108.9	6.8
1990	2857.0	2.6	3474.5	7.6
1991	3425.0	2.8	3045.7	3.5
1992	3054.9	1.5	12,840.2	8.8
1993	3437.3	1.6	13,952.4	8.4
1994	3818.8	1.9	13,837.0	8.5
1995	15512.0	1.6	88,349.9	11.7
1996	18020.4	1.3	75,954.2	13.5
1997	19,26.1	1.6	100,728.3	11.9
1998	16338.9	2.2	102,165.1	16.0
1999	16394.9	1.4	103,489.8	15.8
Average growth rate				
1970-1985	7.8	7.4	26.1	12.7
1986-1993	54.0	3.1	62.0	8.5
1994-1999	54.4	1.7	98.2	12.9

Source: Federal Office of Statistics Lagos.

Appendix III: Custom duty rate for some selected items

No	Item	Tariff rates
1	Cereals	150
2	Maize, potato & cassava starch	40
3	Cane sugar	1
4	Sugars	10
5	Granite (crude oil) (>300mt)	10
6	Cut and polished granite	15
7	Gypsum (200,000,000 tones)	15
8	Plastics of pairs	150
9	Dolomite (16.Smt)	5
10	Iron ore concrete	5
11	Tin metal and alloys	15
12	Sulphur	10
13	Sulphuric acid	15
14	Phosphorus	10
15	Phosphorus acid	10
16	Primary forms of plastic	10
17	Natural rubber	15
18	Rubber latex	10
19	Textile fabrics	45
20	Furniture and furniture products	65

Source: Aliyu, A. (1998: 72)

Globalization: effects on industrial productivity in Nigeria

– Nathaniel C. Ozigbo

Introduction

The purpose of this chapter is to provide basic information on the effects of globalization on industrial productivity in Nigeria. Studies of this kind are scanty in less developed countries. Yet their importance can hardly be over-emphasized. For not only do they provide the basis for international comparison of industrial structures, they also provide basis for following the process of industrialization of less developed countries, while at the same time provide the necessary data for policy in this vital sector.

The term globalization has acquired considerable emotive force. Some scholars view it as a process that is beneficial, a key to future world economic development as well as inevitable and irreversible. Others regard it with hostility, even fear believing it increases inequality within and between nations, threatens employment/living standards and thwarts social progress. In reality globalization offers extensive opportunities for worldwide development, but it is not progressing evenly. Some countries are becoming integrated into the global economy more quickly than others. There is nothing mysterious about globalization. The term has come into common usage since the 1980s, reflecting technological advances that have made it easier and quicker to compete in international transactions, both trade and financial flows. In fact, the whole world is now one market place as a result of technological advancement, sophistication in information sciences and computer technology. Individual and corporate entities in different nations have been brought closer and their activities/interactions have become more co-ordinated than hitherto. While the increasing trend in globalization has its merits, it has nevertheless escalated across national borders, the rate as well as the level of criminal activities as drug trafficking, money laundering, advance fee fraud, among others. The spread of these crimes has generated great concern for government because of its implications for national, economic and social development. Globalization has made the flow of funds easier, while easy flow of money has consequently led to the escalation in the levels of money laundering activities.

However, to what extent has globalization, the increasing international integration of markets for goods, factors and technology affected industrial productivity in Nigeria? This chapter attempts to address this issue focusing particularly on the effects of globalization on industrial productivity gains in Nigeria.

This chapter is divided into four sections. Section one is basically introductory and gives the thrust of the study. Section two discusses the conceptual framework of the Nigerian economy, which falls within the realm of development economics. It defines the characteristics of the economy and the institutional arrangements. Section three examines the industrial structure of the Nigerian economy and discusses different attributes associated with the various stages of industrial transformation. Section four focuses on the effects of globalization on the industrial productivity gains and lastly the conclusions.

This chapter cannot hope to clear up all the issues relating to globalization and productivity gains in Nigeria, as it is limited to a number of constraints. The most important of the limitation is statistical information, which in the sector is incomplete and in some cases difficult to access. It is hoped that subsequent editions of this book will address the data problem associated with the effects of globalization on industrial productivity in Nigeria.

Conceptual framework of the Nigerian economy

Nigeria is the single largest geographical unit in West Africa. It occupies a land area of 923,768 square kilometres situated between longitude 30 and 150 East and Latitude 40 and 140 North. The country is bounded on the west by the Republic of Benin, on the East by the Cameroon Republic, on the North by the Niger and Chad Republic and on the South by a vast coastline of the Atlantic Ocean measuring about 800 km known as the Gulf of Guinea. Climatically, there are two major seasons in Nigeria, the wet and dry seasons. However, there are variations and seasonal patterns that are characteristically humid with substantial rainfall in the south to the north that is dry with little rainfall.

Like most African countries, the Nigerian economy is characterized by dualistic production systems whereby traditional/informal or curb markets systems coexist with modern or formal systems. The modern system is more productive and efficient owing to the utilization of modern production techniques, which permit a very few number of workers to produce for commercial purposes and to cater for the domestic consumption as well as for exports. Large number of informal small enterprises and a few formal modern firms characterizes the structure of industrial sector. According to report from Federal Office of Statistics (FOS, 1992) defined industrial establishment as an economic unit, under a single ownership, which engages in one or predominantly one kind of economic activity at a single location.

Based on the above definition, the size of Nigeria's industrial sector was put at 61,289 establishments, each employing more than five employees. While comprehensive and current data are not available, there are indications that small and medium scale enterprises account for about 70 per cent of industrial employment. The small-scale enterprises tend to be rural based while the medium scale enterprises produce in urban areas in competition with numerous micro enterprises. The Nigerian medium scale enterprises are in a transitional state with production techniques characterized by organized factory-type processing of more complex goods. They employ relatively high technology but unlike large scale enterprises are less capital intensive. Access to technology is not a major constraint they are able to employ technical specialists to install equipment and train employees.

The large enterprises are the modern factories, using the state of the art technologies and mass-producing for both the domestic and export markets. The analysis of industrial structure by size shows that small-scale enterprises constituted 65.5 %, while the medium and large-scale enterprises constituted 32.0 and 2.5 % respectively. Also, in terms of output, small-scale enterprises contributed 85.0 per cent while the medium and large-scale enterprises contributed 10.0 and 5.0 per cent respectively.

According to the studies conducted by the research department of the Central Bank of Nigeria indicated that aggregate industrial output, which fell in the proceeding two years, recorded a modest recovery in year 2001. The estimated index of industrial production at 139.0 (1985 = 100) grew by 7.7 % in year 2001. The factors that influenced the structural changes and performance of industrial, sector included government intervention, inward looking strategy and protectionism. As in other developing economics, the main objectives set by the industrial planners in Nigeria include the desire to achieve increase in the share of manufacturing contribution to the GDP, replacement of imports with locally produced goods, innovativeness, industrial dispersal and employment generation. The performance of the industrial sector is therefore assessed employing criteria such as its share (value added) in GDP, industrial production index, which reflects changes in the level of aggregate output relative to a specific base year period and plant capacity utilization rates. Other yardsticks include the growth and diversity of industrial imports, degree of industrial dispersal, employment generation, level of local raw materials utilization, foreign exchange saving and industrial self-sufficiency. Most investment incentives provided by government were targeted at achieving higher production and greater revenues in the medium to long run.

Industrialization process in Nigeria

The extent to which industrialization contributes to economic development in general and to increased employment and a healthy balance of payments in particular depends, on the type of strategies and policies pursued.

This study and others show clearly that the country has now reached a structural turning point at which far-reaching measures are required to raise the level of national value added from industrial activities through greater linkages. Such a rise will minimize import requirements, avoid high inflationary rates and quicken the period of infant-industry status.

There is obviously great need for a change, possibly radical in the strategies and policies pursued. This change should begin right away for as the Mexican experience shows, "the later an economy switches from industrial import substitution to export promotion, the more strenuous the necessary structural change becomes."

It is perhaps appropriate that a review of the structure of the industry in Nigeria should begin with some introductory remarks on the appeal of industrialization as a necessary ingredient of economic policy. In Nigeria, industrialization has, by and large become synonymous with development. Modern industry has provided employment for the surplus and under-utilized labour from the agricultural sector and has raised the national average productivity of the workers, thereby contributing an increasing proportion of the gross national product. It also has superior linkage effects.

Modern industry as Rostow (1956) has pointed out, "a necessary condition for take-off into sustaining growth." It is important to recognise that the imperative for energizing the industrial transformation in the country, particularly since over a decade age may not be regarded as a peculiarity of Nigeria alone. In fact, the on-going globalization trend has reinforced the growing debate on common markets, free trade areas and the need for a new international economy order. As a consequence of globalization trend, a new World Trade Organization (WTO) was established in 1995 to supersede the earlier General Agreement on Tariffs and Trade (GATT). Also, there exists the formation of the North American Free Trade Agreement (NAFTA) zone. These developments raise the suspicion that there could be the possibility of transforming the trade blocs into cauldrons of hostility that could culminate in socio-economic and industrial war, particularly against third world countries, Nigeria included.

The important question, at this stage relates to whether Nigeria in its process of industrialization to create incentives to save and allow for the inflow of investible funds on the basis of efficient resource allocation within the ongoing processes of globalization coupled with economic liberalization and deregulation paradigms.

However, the imperative for energizing the industrial transformation in Nigeria is to create a conducive environment under which there would be free inflow of foreign investible funds. This could be possible if the current industrial environment changes to one whose enabling environment encourages industrial policy instruments that make Nigeria a least cost industrial producer. This suggests something drastic must be done policy-wise to modify the existing high bank-lending rate to make it supportive to the industrialization process. This suggests again that in the process of energizing the industrial transformation of the Nigerian economy that the Central Bank of Nigeria has a major role to play in sanitizing the banking system to make for efficiency and low cost industrial production.

Similarly, the government owes it a duty to make the industrial environment attractive and perfect for operation. These could be attained through adequate guaranteed supply of utilities to all users, establishment of wage structures to raise effective demand for goods/services and creating a condition for sustaining democratic government in the country. The government should put up prudent strategies to diversity Nigeria's export base and policy efforts must emphasis the need to minimize the large currency depreciation, which could lead to a further decline in terms of trade.

To digress a little bit, traditionally, the study of industrial transformation has been undertaken for purposes of policies aimed at maintaining competition, thereby ensuring the full benefit of the market system. Such policies are devised either to prevent or minimize deviations from the accepted competitive norm or to minimize the abuses where for one reason or another, no attempt is made to prevent monopoly or collusion among firms. The United States and Britain afford good examples of attempts to ensure the benefits of free market systems through different approaches.

Against this background, the Nigerian government must focus on accelerating the implementation of export diversification initiatives. Such diversification strategies must be comprehensive. That is, such policy instruments must emphasize both the supply and demand sides of the production process. The supply side must focus for success on research and development, human capital development and marketing strategies that facilitate an expanded range and improved quality of exportable commodities.

On the demand side, policy strategies must be directed at expanding domestic, regional and western markets and thereby increasing market share. It is evident that radical changes in policy are required to effect the type of structural changes necessary in Nigeria's industrial sector.

Effects of globalization on industrial productivity

Technological innovations and the dismantling of trade barriers have contributed to an acceleration of growth in global trade. From various studies, one could see that globalization which accompany technological innovations have the intention of generating productivity gains by reducing transaction costs. As a result of globalization, industries can expect productivity gains through improved systems for procurement and inventory control and reduced costs of intermediation and sales transactions, as well as through more rapid diffusion of technology. For instance, the rise in Nigerian labour productivity growth from 1.5 % per year form 1990 – 1995 to nearly 2.6 % per year in the late 1990s was closely tied to innovations in information technology in the global market. In essence, there are three principal sources of productivity gains in Nigeria as a result of globalization and improved information technology. These include capital deepening, represented by increases in the amount of plant and equipment per worker, improvement in technology and in the organization of the production process.

Scholars in developed economies emphasizes that productivity may slow initially because of costs associated with obtaining and implementing the new technology as well as increased scrap rates, reflecting more rapid obsolescence of old capital. The scholars pinpointed that the speed of the recovery in productivity is determined by factors such as the slope of the learning curve and the time required for the complete replacement of older technologies.

In Nigerian situation, the extensive research on assessing productivity gains in different sectors of the economy has revealed severe measurement problems. However, Ajakaiye and Ayodele (2000) stress the importance of industry-level analysis in examining past trends in Nigerian productivity growth. They emphasized that until these information gaps are addressed, evaluating the spread of Information Technology gains in productivity to other sectors will remain an open questions.

While the transmission of information productivity gains to the service sector has not materialized fully, it is clear that the demand for Information technology goods has remained strong, making it reasonable to expect that the gains in information technology productivity will continue to contribute positively to overall productivity growth in Nigeria for some time. Recent evidence suggests that productivity appears to be increasing outside of information technology sectors. For instance, non-manufacturing productivity has increased noticeably since mid 1999 and productivity in retail activity has been on the upswing. If these indicators reflect the on set of information technology penetration into the production processes of other sectors, then strong productivity growth could continue for some time. What it means is that government should as a matter of priority, provide the necessary congenial social and economic environment with which the application of the new technology will be feasible. Given such enabling environment, adoption of Information technology will obviously have a multiplier effect on economic development, as it will help to attract funds outside the system so that they can be properly channelled into the areas of priority. Given the role technology has played in the modernization of the Nigerian economy especially the banking sector in terms of development of new banking system as well as strategic management in the emerging market economies, there is no doubt that the future of the industrial sector will be technology-driven. Indeed, with the emergence of the global digital economy and increased internationalization and competition,

Nigerian Industrial sector must enlarge and deepen their technological base, if they are to be viable domestically and competitive internationally.

Conclusion

Nigerian industrial sector is gradually and slowly waking up to Information Technology that is expected to lead them to the global world through Internet connectivity. Undoubtedly, Nigeria's industrial sector is the most intensive user of introductory technology in the country and they are expected to play an important role in spearheading expended and aggressive user of Information Technology.

As noted earlier, the future of the Nigerian industrial sector will be driven by technology. As Nigerian industrial sector intensify efforts to enhance their technology acquisition and capability, there is need for proper, phased and co-ordinated implementation of automation schemes. Against this backdrop and in spite of well-known financial, infrastructural and cultural constraints, industrial sector can still attain automation of their operations through properly sequenced and collaborative efforts aimed primarily at developing the skills that already exist locally. This would not only increase local value-added but will serve to reduce costs.

In spite of the numerous benefits derivable from the current wave of globalization, which has transformed the contours of the industrial and other sectors, the development poses many challenges for Nigerian Industrial sector. With globalization, there is bound to be an increased competition as well as risk exposures in industries, which no doubt poses challenges to all the stakeholders in the industrial sector and the economy as a whole. Also, the openness of the Nigerian economy to international capital markets makes it more exposed to shocks originating from abroad, which are then transmitted through international capital flows.

As a result of globalization, the stability of the industrial sector may be threatened. For instance, greater market liberalization and internationalization go hand in hand with greater risk of potential disruptions that originates in or is transmitted through financial markets. In Nigeria, the operational activities of most industries are increasingly becoming more sophisticated as advancement in technologies offer industries a variety of options for new product development and the chance for the continuous exploitation of new opportunities in a dynamic environment. With the democratization of governance in the country and the liberalization of the financial system, more industries including foreign ones are likely to be licensed. With this development, it is expected that there would emerge better harmonization and standards amongst the various sub-sectors of the nation's industrial sector than hitherto and pave way for an efficient and effective industrial system in the country.

Even though globalization poses various challenges, it has provided strong impetus for industrial innovation. That is, the operational activities of industries are becoming increasingly sophisticated as the new technologies under the new dispensation offer industries a variety of options.

Finally, as a result of globalization, cross-country capital flows are growing rapidly and domestic systems are consequently exposed to shock emanating form abroad. Such flows can now be large enough to pose some significant problems for industrial, financial and economic stability in the country. Such flows might heightened the risk of both industrial and financial crisis.

References

Adenikinju, A and L. Chete (1995) "Productivity and Growth in Nigeria Manufacturing," *African Journal of Economic Policy*, Vol. 2 No. 1.

Akeredolu-Ale, E.O. (1972) "The Nigeria's Industrialization Process," *The Nigerian Journal of Economics and Social Studies*, Vol. 14, No. 1, pp. 109–120.

Arema, J. A. (1991) "Industrial Development Co-ordinating Committee, and Foreign Private Investment in Nigeria," *Bullion*, Publication of Central Bank of Nigeria, vol. 29, No. 4.

Bain, J. S. (1959) *Industrial Organization*, New York, John Wiley and Sons Inc., p. 7.

Berman, E. and E. Grilliches (1994) "Changes in the Demand for Skilled Labour Within United States Manufacturing: Evidence from the Annual Survey of Manufactures," *Quarterly Journal of Economics*, Vol. 109, May, pp. 367–97.

Borjas, G. L. and L. Katz (1992) *On the Labour Market, Effects of Immigration and Trade, Economic Consequences for the United States and Source Areas*, Chicago, University of Chicago Press.

Cronin Mary, J. (1995) *Doing more Business on the Internet*, 2nd edition, New York, Van Nostrand Reinhold.

Federal Republic of Nigeria (1988) *Industrial Policy of Nigeria (Policies, Incentives, Guidelines and Institutions Framework)*, Federal Ministry of Industries, Abuja.

Feldstein M. and H. Charles (1980) "Domestic Savings and International Capital Flows," *Economic Journal*, Vol. 90, June, pp. 314–29.

Heldman, R. K. (1992) *Global Telecommunications: Layered Networks, Layered Services*, New York, McGraw-Hill, Inc.

Helpman E. and Krugman (1983) *Market Structure and Foreign Trade, Increasing Returns, Imperfect Competition and the International Economy*, Cambridge, Massachusetts, MIT Press.

Maurice, L. N. (1997) "Globalization: Its Threats and Opportunities," Address to Chartered Institute of Company Secretariat in Australia, Sydney.

Olu, Ajakaiye and A.S. Ayodele (2000) "The Imperative for Energizing Industrial Transformation in Nigeria," *Bullion*, Publication of the Central Bank of Nigeria, vol. 24, No. 2, April/June.

World Bank (1990) "Industrial Sector Report Restructuring Policies for Competitiveness and Export Growth," Vol. 11, March, No. 8868.

8

Nigeria from indigenization to globalization

– Sule Magaji

Introduction

The history of Nigeria shows that the country's relationship with outside world passed through slave trade era, the so-called legitimate trade, the eventual imposition of colonial administration and the colonial economic policy and the de-colonisation of the Nigerian economy through indigenization policy. Paradoxically the country introduced the policy to attract foreign investment, the privatization and commercialisation policy, and now the globalization policy. This shows that there is a cycle in economy policy from indigenization to globalization.

The chapter is classified into eight sections. These sections are introduction, indigenization and globalization; historical perspective, indigenization policy, policy to attract foreign direct investment, and the privatization policy. Others are the globalization policy, recommendations and conclusion.

The chapter shows that Nigeria is tied to the metropolitan countries and therefore, any economic policy pursued by the mother countries invariably has impact on the Nigerian economy. It shows again that globalization would not augur well for Nigeria. On the contrary it is just a harbinger of more unemployment, widening of the gap between the 'haves' and the 'have nots' at both national and international levels.

Trade protection was not prominent in Nigeria long before the colonial era. Nigeria's contact with colonialists was only at the end of nineteenth century when the corn law of 1846 was abolished and the process of trade liberalisation has began in Europe (Egware, 1998). As a result of liberalisation the share of exports in world output increased sharply as from 1913 due largely to reduced tariff and reduced transportation cost (Irwin, 1993; Bairoch and Kozul-Wright, 1996).

Although the classical gold standard prevailed before the first European war or the inter-imperialists war, but the network of bilateral commercial treaties constituted a liberal multi-lateral trade regime. At the period after the second European war, the story was different in Nigeria. The scramble for Nigeria by the colonialists made trade arrangement between Nigeria and British an imposed bilateral one. Nigeria specialised in primary product exports in exchange for British manufactured products.

At the time when regional economic integration was at peak, Nigeria was not even an independent nation and so the imposed bilateral trade continued. As a quick device to throw away the yoke of economic exploitation, Nigeria in particular, resorted to nationalism (Awolabi, 1998). This action led to the attainment of political independence by the country. With political independence, the desire for economic independence motivated government to embark on indigenization policy. This policy was a short-lived one as a result of gross inadequacy of saving generating ability of the economy. Mismanagement, corruption and general inefficiency further made the government to relinquish some of its economic venture to private sector and also solicit for foreign direct investment (FDI).

The current advances on information technology, the liberal economic philosophy embodied in the worldwide structural adjustment programmes sweeping both the developed and developing economies, and the liberalization of world trades, have resulted in the increasing globalization of world production processes as well as financial institutions and markets.

Nigeria's indigenization policy

Indigenization deals with the process of encouraging indigenous private entrepreneur. Indigenization is of different types namely, indigenization of ownership, and indigenization of control. The basis of indigenization was to attain economic independence. As industries are engine of economic growth and development, the control should be in the hands of indigenous people.

Throughout the colonial period and ten years after independence multinational corporations dominated Nigeria. Indigenization policy was Nigeria's response to the challenge of economic hegemony by the multinational corporations. The indigenization policy took three stages and has varied in the extent of alienation of foreign investors as well as in the involvement and participation of indigenous entrepreneurs.

The first stage of indigenization covered the period between 1962 and 1972, during which the government embarked upon a gradual control of the economy through increase capitalisation of public corporations and control of public utilities to the exclusion of private sector. This was achieved through increasing legal regulations of the activities of private investors as well as increasing equity participation of government in strategic sectors of the economy. At this stage, the 1968 Company Decree; the 1969 Banking Decree; the Expatriate Allocation Board of 1966; and the Exchange Control Order of 1971 collectively re-sharpened the legal environment for business.

The second stage involves two major developments, namely, the promulgation of Indigenization Decree or the Nigerian Enterprises Promotion Decree of 1972 which came into effect in April 1974, and the Industrial Enterprises Panel appointed in 1975. The major goal of this stage was the Nigerianization of ownership and control of strategic industries to ensure that Nigerians determine the economic destiny of the country. However, both aliens and indigenous business exploited a number of loopholes in the decree. The loopholes include exemption granted by the commission of industries to some enterprises, ambiguous definition of Nigerian citizens or associations by the Decree according to which OAU members were citizens, lack of clearly set down procedures for sale of business and false declaration of assets by foreign companies.

The third stage attempted to address the problems of second stage. Review was made of the 1972 Decree and the recommendation of the review panel formed the basis of the 1977 indigenization decree. As a result of the review, the federal government has at least 60 per cent of ten equity participation of strategic companies and in terms of management; Nigerians were appointed as directors of most of the companies.

However, the indigenization policy was not able to count chickens from eggs laid. This was as a result of continued alien manoeuvres that prolonged their period of non-compliance, for in management positions which competent Nigerians were available and high income inequity caused by concentration of wealth in the hands of few Nigeria elite. Perhaps these problems necessitate policy changes in ownership and investment.

The major impacts of indigenization policy are negative in nature. One was the emergence of rich elites who amassed wealth as a result of holding higher positions in the government on investments. This creates a polarized social stratification with the poor people pushed to the bottom of the ladder. Two, was the creation of fear for foreign investors to make any meaningful investment in the future.

Policy to attract foreign direct investment (FDI)

As we highlighted above, the first dramatic policy change against the loss of economic independence was indigenization. However, a circle was made back to the former policy of allowing foreigners to have a say in the domestic economy especially through FDI. Policy to attract FDI seemed desirable because domestic savings potential of Nigeria, as a result of high income inequality was found inadequate to provide the needed apparatus upon which a solid foundation for sustainable investment could be laid. This in particular necessitated the need to source alternative sources of funding domestic investment expenditure both in the private and public sectors of the economy. Indeed the colonial orientation of Nigeria and the deliberate distortionary economic structure put in place that orient Nigeria towards primary products production and the entrenchment of importation syndrome, accounted for the dearth of savings.

The inadequacy of domestic savings in the 1980s had led to renewed attention being given to FDI as a source of finance for industrial development in Nigeria. Once viewed as a mechanism of imperialists penetration into a victim country (Magaji, 2000). FDI is now seen as an important source of long term capital and as a means of achieving employment, skills, technology and export growth. Unlike loans, which must be financed regardless of the productivity of the capital, services on FDI are tied to the capital performance of the business ventures, which gives the foreign investor a stronger interest in how his funds are used. Joint ventures are also seen as an alternative to obstacles to market access, management skills acquisition, new technology and foreign exchange for Nigeria's business.

As a place to invest, Nigeria continues to be less attractive than industrial countries. Difficulties with the availability of local inputs, inability to import necessary production goods, restriction on the mobility of personnel and exchange regulations are typical of the problems that foreign inventors face in Nigeria. To these must be added the heightened risk perceptions that foreign investors have of Nigeria. Others of continuing importance are unpredictability of government behaviour when political institutions are weakened, unstable macro-economic environment, dilapidated economic and social infrastructures, insecurity of life and property and inefficient banking and financial system.

Empirical result of Salako and Adebusuyi (2001) showed that external debt ratio reflected an *a priori* expectation that a debt ridden country will not be able to attract foreign investors. Their result showed that when the external debt ratio rises by one per cent, the inflow of FDI will reduce by about 15 per cent. Obadan (1994) cited in Salako and Adebusuyi also noted that high rate of inflation reduces international competitiveness of exports, foreign exchange earning and put pressure on current account and exchange rates. These create an adverse investment climate. As a result of these problems, the policy to attract FDI has little impact on the economy.

The privatization policy

Privatization is seen as policy change that enlarges the scope for private enterprises to compete with state owned enterprises, or ones that may cause state enterprises to operate like private enterprises. It is significant to note that after the attainment of political independence and the need to establish import substitution industries, it became obvious that it was only the government that could provide enough capital to venture into certain kinds of economic activities. Financed by government include the petroleum industry, agricultural sub-sectors such as the River Basin Development Authorities, National Diaries Companies and National Fertiliser Company. Other areas of interest to the government included the Nigeria Railway Corporation, the Nigeria Airways, the Nigeria Telecommunication Services, Nigeria Port Authority, the National Electric Power Authority and many others.

It now amounted to double standard for a country that complained of lack of domestic savings and therefore pursing a policy to attract FDI to now embark on privatization of government enterprises to domestic investors. Since the domestic investors have no enough capital to privatization would only be successful with the collaboration of foreign and domestic inventors. In any case there is a cycle in economic policy from indigenization to neo-colonialization.

Many different goals motivated government to embark on privatization. These goals include the need to improve government cash flows, enhancing the efficiency of state enterprises and curbing the power of labour unions in these public sector enterprises. Two factors are responsible for privatization in Nigeria. The factors are economic and socio-political.

From economic point of view, it is clear that state owned enterprises survives on state funding in the form of subventions, grants, subsidised loans and favoured patronage of their products or services by the government. The concept of managerial efficiency is usually not considered in the operational framework of most state owned enterprises. This stems from the fact that profit is not the major goal and state funding is readily available to serve as a cushion on the negative impact of loss. More so, production function is structured in such a way that productive efficiency, cost minimisation and competitive quality of products is not adhered to. The effect of these negative operational characteristics made such enterprises economically unviable and hence the need to either completely or fully transfer their ownership to private sector.

From socio-political point of view, a closely associated malaise of state owned enterprises is their location in areas that are economically sub-optimal to produce and managed by incompetent managers appointed based on their political cleavages or ethnic background. The managers mostly incompetent and unqualified know little about productive efficiency, competitiveness and cost minimisation. With this problem, privatization would be about diluted ownership to include new managers or complete transferred ownership to new private entrepreneurs.

Although privatization policy seem to be relevant at least from the two points of view we analysed, but the sale or lease of a government firms can leave the economy worse off if intensive concessions have to be extended to the buyers. Again the immediate social cost of privatization can be severe on the Nigerian economy. This is because the country has no plan for lid off workers, no retraining and re-deployment schemes, and there is poor record of placing workers because of economic recession. Privatization would further compound the problem of widening gap between the have and the have not within the country with associated social problems of high level crime.

Nigeria and the globalization policy

Globalization is not a new phenomenon. The colonial era provided a more integrated world economy controlled by the metropolitan countries. However, the present trend of globalization differs from the earlier one. Participation in the earlier one was essentially shallow although more destructive due to the unfavourable terms of trade against Nigeria whose exports were exclusively primary products. The present globalization is viewed as a process of integrating economic decision making such as the consumption, investment, and saving process all across the world. It is a process of creating a global market place in which, increasingly all nations are forced to participate. Key elements of this process are: the interconnection of sovereign nations through trade and capital flows, harmonisation of the economic rules that govern relationships between these sovereign nations, creating structures to support and facilitate dependence and interconnection and creation of global market places (Kwanashi 1998). Globalization may therefore, be seen as a process of interdependence among nations in all aspects of life but most importantly economic.

Globalization is essential because the western nations seeking more profitable outlets need the integration of the world economy and access to all part of the world. The process of achieving this noble goal was through regionalization, trade liberalization, expansion of multinational corporations, international financial markets, deregulation of world economy and international financial institutions.

Regionalization was aimed at providing a common market to the exclusion of others so as to make a particular region strong to compete around the world. As the regional markets reached their limits, the focus shifted to regional blocks collectively doing business with the outside world. The establishment of regional markets was therefore, deliberate strategies by the industrialised world to maintain their hegemony over the less industrialised nations.

As the regional markets of the industrial nations gained strength, the quest was for trade liberalisation, the developing countries emerging industries must collapse to the advantage of stronger western industries. Western countries encouraged trade liberalisation by putting it as a condition of getting foreign finance and better foreign relationship.

From regionalization, to trade liberalisation and thence to strong flourishing of multinational companies (MNCs) to less developed countries. This was stimulated by the desire of less developed countries to attract foreign investors. The MNCs have been major vehicle for globalization of manufacturing, in which relatively cheap labour in developing countries has been equipped with capital and modern technique of production. The western nations benefits from

MNCs activities because the companies made great profits even when majority in the host countries lived below the poverty line.

The international financial market also stimulates the globalization process. The globalization of financial markets entails more gains for private capital, which can now flow around the globe in search of high interest. Finance capital today responds rapidly to new profit opportunities. However, the industrial countries have more opportunities to get the lion share of global savings for their economic activities. This is because finance is attracted on the basis of sound economic fundamentals.

The process of globalization is also to be accomplished with the realisation of goals of the institutional agents of globalization. These institutions include the World Bank, the International Monetary Fund (1MF) and the World Trade Organisation. These institutions collectively aimed at facilitating global economy through trade liberalisation, deregulation of economies, dispute settlement mechanism for the conduct of international trade, etc. (Egware, 1988).

Why Nigeria embraced globalization

One glaring happening is that yet, there is a cycle in economic policy from indigenization to globalization. Most of the arguments put forward in defence of globalization is that countries of the world benefit by harnessing the resulting opportunities to the proper development of their material and human endowment. In general, as Nemedia (1998) highlighted, globalization brings about increase in competitive production structures, which leads to more efficiency and productivity gains; increases in world output as a result of world specialisation with each nation only producing at a comparative cost advantage; improved market access; greater financial intermediation; transfer of technology and managerial capacity building.

But Nigeria is inferior economically. It cannot withstand the competition of international market. As shown in Table 1, the country lagged behind other African countries in terms of GDP growth rate. The country has also shown nothing to reckon with in the industrial sector. It has averaged annual growth rate of 1.7% between 1990-1999 as against 4.8% recorded in Ghana.

Nigeria is embracing globalization blindly just as the way it embraced so many economic policies of the past, especially the economic deregulation, without analysing the consequences. Questions such as how competitive is our financial sector? How volatile is international financial market? How strong is Nigeria's state of technology and managerial know-how? And how elastic is the demand of Nigeria's product in the world market, etc. need to be answered.

Firstly, globalization will leave Nigeria's banking and finance sector in a weak competitive position due to lack of required degree of sophistication on the production of managers, inferior level of technology, and poor infrastructural facilities for banking and finance operation.

Secondly, the volatile nature of international financial markets can cause more volatility of Nigeria's financial system and promote capital flight, with accompanying problems of balance of payment as well as dilemma for monetary and exchange rate policies.

Thirdly, Nigeria runs the risk of marginalisation in the real market due to poor technological developments and lack of managerial know-how. This will lead to adverse term of trade.

Fourthly, low-income elasticity of demand for primary commodities of Nigeria coupled with the declining intensity of raw materials use in manufacturing production process means that globalization will send the country's economy to depression.

Table 1: Comparative average annual growth rates of selected developing countries

Countries	GDP		Agriculture value added		Industry value added		Services value added		Gross domestic investment
	1980 to 1990	*1990 to 1999*	*1980 to 1990*	*1990 to 1999*	*1980 to 1990*	*1990 to 1999*	*1980 to 1990*	*1990 to 1999*	*1990 to 1999*
Angola	3.4	0.8	0.5	-3.1	6.4	4.2	1.8	-3.4	12.0
Burkina Faso	3.6	3.8	3.1	3.5	3.8	3.9	4.6	3.5	4.8
Chad	6.1	2.3	2.3	4.9	8.1	2.2	6.7	0.8	4.4
Ghana	3.0	4.3	1.0	3A	3.3	4.8	5.7	5.0	4.2
Kenya	4.2	2.2	3.3	1.4	3.9	1.9	3.3	4A	4.9
Nigeria	1.6	2.4	3.3	2.9	-1.1	1.7	3.7	3.1	5.8

Source: World Development Report 2000/2001

Lastly, globalization is accompanied with trade liberalisation and total economic deregulation. This means that the lack of competitive nature of Nigeria's industries will make the country a dumping ground of foreign product and render the domestic currency worthless vis-à-vis the other currencies of the world. This is a harbinger of low productivity, mass unemployment, falling investment and income, falling standard of living, high level of crime and general economic stagnation.

Summary, recommendation and conclusion

Review of policies above showed that there is a trend in economic programmes in Nigeria. Each policy and programme in the country is governed by the global economic trend. What is clear is that Nigeria embraces most economic policies spearheaded by industrial nations with optimism.

The dramatic changes in economic policies of Nigeria were mainly caused by the influence of industrialised countries. Throughout the history of Nigeria's foreign economic relationship, the country was not interested in knowing how the gains from the proceeds of international economic policies are shared. For example Nigeria only reacted against foreign economic domination through indigenization when the damages of foreign control were already been made. the indigenization policy was not successful because the structures of the economy was moulded toward serving western industries. As a result of lack of economic empowerment of the country caused by unequal terms of trade in international exchange, Nigeria resorted to re-inviting foreign investors to come back and invest, and also to subject the country to total deregulation in order to suit the globalization policy.

Lastly, we have seen that globalization will not augur well for Nigeria. This is because the country specialises in primary product production. Again, technological backwardness of Nigeria means that it cannot compete in the world market. As a result of these problems Nigeria will be marginalized in a globalized economy. The country's economy will continue as stagnant, and the long unequal terms of trade in international transactions will continue.

Since as we observed, Nigeria will remain an infant in a globalized economy, the country would remain as an appendage of industrialized nations. Nigeria would have to make effort to catch up through selective control in international trade, infrastructural development, motivation of local savings and investments, and orientation towards patronage in favour of Nigeria's made products. The country should not compromise unemployment, fall in living standard, and loss of economic independence at the expense of globalization.

Highlight of this topic show that there is a cycle in economic policy in Nigeria from indigenization to globalization: what is clear is that Nigeria embraces most economic policies pursued by industrial nations with all optimism without analysing their consequences. This in most cases leaves Nigeria at a disadvantage when it comes to sharing of the gains. In the case of globalization it is nothing but a subtle and ingenious imperialism.

Reference

David, F.C. and Nixson (1986) *Economic of Change in less Developed Countries*, 2nd ed., Philip Acan Publishers Ltd, Oxford.

Egware, L.E. (1998) "Institutional Agents of Globalization," *CBNE&F Review*, vol. 36

Frank, R.R. (1978) *International Trade and Investment* (4th Ed.) South-Western Publishing Co. Cincinnati, Ohio

Gulemo, et al C.A. (1996) "Inflows of Capital to Developing Countries in the 1990s," *Journal of Economic Perspectives*, Vol. 10, No. 2

International Monetary Fund (1997) "Globalization. Opportunities and Challenges," *World Economic Outlook*, May

Kwanashie, M. (1998) "Concept and Process of Globalization," *Economic and Financial Review*, Vol.36

Magaji, 5. (2000) "Nigeria and Foreign Debt: The Desire for Economic Development Versus Imperialism," *Journal of Economics and Allied Field*, Vol. 1 No. 1 September.

Michael, C. (1997) "Globalization and its challenges for Germany. Europe and the IMF," in *The Challenges of Globalization in an Interdependent World Economy*, IMF Washington, DC

Nemedia, C.E. (1998) "Merits and Demerits of Globalization," *CBNEF Review*, Vol. 36

Offiong, D.A. (1980) *Imperialism and Dependency*, Fourth Dimension Publishers, Enugu.

Ogbu, S. O. (2000) "Privatization and Commercialisation Programme in Nigeria: A Critical Analysis," *Journal of Economics and Allied Fields*, Vol. 1 No. 1 September.

Oloyede, G. (1998) "Regional Political and Economic Groupings as Vehicles for Globalization," *CBN Economic and Finance Review* Vol. 36.

Salako, H. A. and B. S. Adebusuyi (2001) "Determinants of Foreign Direct Investment in Nigeria: An Empirical Investigation," *CBN Econ. & Fin. Review*, Vol. 39:1

Usman, S. (1998) "Planning and Phasing the Privatization of Key Enterprises in Nigeria," Preceding of the National Seminar on Privatization, held at NICON Hotel, Abuja

Tibor, 5. (1958) *Economic Theory and Western European Integration*, Chiwin University Books, London

Wilfred, G. (1988) *Economic Policy Coordination*. IIME, Washington DC

World Bank (2001) *World Development Report 2000/2001*, Oxford University Press.

9

Privatization in a globalized context: the Nigerian experience

– Nazifi Abdullahi Darma

Introduction

The State ownership and control of economic enterprises engaged in directly productive activities in most countries of the world is due to the structural rigidities and distortions of the market resulting in its failure. More particularly in the case of developing countries the need to lay a solid foundation for sustainable industrialization premised on the import substitution strategy cannot be overemphasized.

Besides pure economic considerations, socio-political factors play a decisive role in determining the nature, location, type and production process of such enterprises in Nigeria. Massive investments manifesting in direct budgetary allocation, grants, subventions and loans were made by the Nigerian state to such state owned economic entities with multiplicity of objectives expected to be achieved in the process. Employment, technological acquisition, regional/sectoral economic balancing and general industrialization drive and take off were some of the arguments in favour of the establishment and funding of these enterprises by the state.

The dramatic fall in the prices of oil as the major foreign exchange earner and revenue contributor for the Nigerian Economy in the early 1980s necessitated a shift in economic management philosophy towards tight and restrictive public expenditure policy. This resulted in massive reduction of budgetary allocation to almost every sector of the economy of which state owned enterprises are not an exception. The state realized that expansive public expenditure programmes resulting from windfall gains in oil prices in the 1980s resulting in white elephant projects and unsustained import syndrome cannot be guaranteed in the face of a dramatic fall in the prices of a mono-revenue earner by the mid 1980s.

Decline in government revenue through the sale of crude petroleum seriously reduced the capacity of the state to continue its expansive public expenditure programme of which financing state enterprises through direct investment, subventions and grants are of central importance. An alternative becomes imperative to secure if the state enterprises are to remain operational.

The emergence of a new dominant economic thinking away from Keynesian economics in favour of neo-liberalism in the early 1980s seriously change economic policy formulation. The neo-liberalists emphasize more the concept of government failure in favour of market mechanism. This coupled with the emergence of conservative "market apologist' regimes in Europe and America together with the continued deterioration in the external finances of developing countries especially non oil exporters, facilitated the application of a universal solution to solve a perceived common problem.

Advancement in information technology, continued consolidation and merger of business conglomerates, Trans-national corporation and the strengthening of regional trading alliances are factors that combined to increase the depth and extent of competition manifesting in the recent globalization trend.

The objectives of the chapter are:

(1) Discussing the theoretical framework for free market capitalism.
(2) Outlining reasons for government intervention in the economy and the emergence of state owned enterprises.
(3) Privatization as a phenomenon associated with globalization.
(4) Discuss whether privatization is achievable in the absence of economic empowerment or not.

The chapter is divided into three parts. Part two discusses neo-liberalism and economic orientation as some of the motivating factors behind globalization and privatization. Part three discusses globalized privatization and the linkage between propagation of globalization and privatization in Nigeria. Part four discusses summary, conclusions and recommendations.

Neo liberalism and economic orientation

The great depression of the 1930s marked a significant turning point in economic policy focus especially in Europe. The *laissez-faire* attitude leading to the general economic crisis was not only an indictment on the structural and functional inadequacies associated with the market, but an opportunity to have a new beginning in economic development with a shift in focus to alternatives ways of resolving the market crises.

Keynesian economics received major boost as an alternative therapy to the general depression that beset Europe and America. Prior to Keynesian economic prescriptions, the dominant economic tool for policy is the classical orthodoxy strongly driven by laissez-faireism and the "say's law" which states that supply creates its own demand. To the classical economists, the only equilibrium position that an economy may experience is the limiting one of full employment compared to the Keynesian view that an economy may indeed be at a position of equilibrium with less than full employment.

To the classical economists, an economy left alone can move towards full employment as it is directed by the invisible hand lending credence to the fact that the economy possesses an automatic self-balancing/adjustment mechanism. Keynesian Economics on the other hand argued that, an economy left on its own may not move towards or attain full employment except through the use of policies to achieve specific macro economic objectives, notable of which are: income, monetary and fiscal policies.

A corner stone of the pre-Keynesian orthodoxy is the quantity theory of money, which emphasized the domineering role of total money supply in determining output, employment, prices and income. To the monetarists who shared a similar view of the pre-Keynesian classical orthodoxy, the quantity of money in circulation is a determinant of aggregate consumption, income and employment though the instrumentality of velocity of circulation.

Keynes on the other hand argued strongly that though there is a relationship between aggregate spending and volume of money in circulation, but the quantity of money is only a factor among several others that determine total spending. Indeed the success of Keynesian economics is amplified by the self-adjusting success of the fiscal policy instruments – government spending and variation in taxation. Most countries in the post depression years realized that, increases in government spending either on directly production activities (DPA) or the provision of social overhead capital (SOC) were vital in moving their economy towards full employment. Taxation and its variation were discovered to be potent tools for increasing or reducing excess disposable income that was in most cases accused of being a causative agent in creating inflationary pressure based on the extra purchasing ability conferred on the consumer.

The policy prescription and adoption success achieved by the industrial world with Keynesian economics in the post recession years was advanced as one of the factors that favour state intervention in economic activities. Other factors include the established industries that are import substituting in nature capable of providing employment, income and technological linkages. The drive towards bridging the income gap that characterized most developing economics in the post independence era and regional/sectoral economic balancing were some of the factors advanced for the emergence of state owned enterprises in Nigeria today as had occurred in other parts of the developing world.

The market failure argument as per its inability to produce goods and assign prices to them, by virtue of their non-rivalry in production and non-excludability in consumption and the manifestation of negative externalities fall within the framework of arguments advanced to justify state enterprises.

Huge public expenditure was used in initiating, financing and consolidating the operations of state owned enterprises in Nigeria with the aim of achieving the aforementioned goals that cannot be delivered by the market.

As discussed earlier, the dependent capitalist orientation of the Nigerian state, expose its vulnerability to externally induced shocks in the global market activities. As the price of oil took a nose-dive in the mid 1980s, a barrel of oil fell to less than $10 dollars, the economy was economically incapacitated to absolve the balance of payment, external debt repayment, budget deficit and general resources allocation shock that accompanied such dramatic fall in the price of the mono revenue earner.

Significantly, the 1980s coincided with a period of political reengineering in the west that precipitated the emergence of conservative neo-liberal political establishments across Europe and United States of America. It is indeed a period characterized by two seemingly distinct, though mutually re-enforcing politico-economic policies termed 'Thatchernomics' and ergonomics strongly ascribed to the then British prime-minister Margaret Thatcher and the United States President Ronald Reagan. Their economic policies framework provided the pillar upon which neo-liberal economics thrived.

Added to this was the wide spread economic recession faced by the world accounted for partly by double digit increases in the price of crude oil which seriously dethrone the balances of most developing countries especially the non-oil exporters. It is even worse for oil producers that were afflicted by the Dutch disease whose economic condition, forced them to seek for short and medium term balance of payment support facilities from the World Bank and the International Monetary Fund (IMF). These two institutions provide such balance of payment facilities through the instrumentality of a programme called structural adjustment programme (SAP) 1986.

Parts of the conditionality of the structural adjustment package include, but not limited to the privatization and commercialization of state owned enterprises that are mainly funded through public expenditure. The major thrust of this conditionality is to free taxpayer's resources that are used to finance the operations of those enterprises for other social uses.

Co-incidentally, most of the balance of payments crisis ridden economies are developing in nature with a strong presence of public sector investment profile in their economic portfolio. These seem to give the unwarranted universality of privatization as a core-package component of the adjustment programme.

The conditions laid down by those international financial institutions popularly referred to as "international agents of anarchy and disorder" were more in tune with the political economy orientation of the major western powers and American being capitalist states and major shareholders in those institutions at the conception, actualization, supervision and implementation of the adjustment programme across the broad spectrum of the political strata that influenced and dominated the direction of lending to the benefiting nation states.

The economic orientation is neo-liberalism – an economic policy framework that postulates itself as a critique of the Keynesian economic prescription with its bias for strong governmental intervention in the economy. The neo-liberal paradigm re-emphasized the classical economic doctrines with modest differences in terms of content and quality. Suffice is to say that the adjustment facility seeking countries were hitherto characterized by the following among other characteristics:

(1) One party/military regimes
(2) Strong element of trade regulation and protection.
(3) A disproportionately strong public sector engaged in directly productive activities.
(4) A regulated foreign exchange market.
(5) Centralized control of prices and resource allocation.
(6) Regulated Interest rate regime.
(7) Widespread support and subsidy schemes economy wide.

The conditionalties being market – oriented in nature seek to re-emphasize the relevance of market in the national economy with a strong emphasis on reducing the extent and level of government intervention in the economy to its minimum. These include:

(1) Trade liberalization and non-protectionism.
(2) Market determined foreign exchange rate.
(3) General economic liberalization and reduced controls.
(4) Privatization and commercialization of government owned enterprises.
(5) Removal of subsidies.
(6) Introduction of cost recovery programme in social services especially health and education.
(7) Commitment to democracy characterized by multiparty structure.

At the core/centre of these conditionalities is the realization of short and long term interest of international capital of wealth accumulation, profiteering and dominance. This is corroborated the more since European municipalities are the major financiers/contributors to the fund of these creditor-institutions.

The nature of international capital today manifesting in the resurgence of neo-liberalism cannot be explained outside the context of its previous hegemony and dominance. Colonialism as ascribed by economic historians to be an outcome of the stiff internal competition associated with domestic markets leading to search for alternative cheaper sources of raw materials and inputs together with the quest for identifying outlets for disposing finished manufactured goods can comfortably be characterized as the initial phase of the globalization process. The resultant effect of this action was the partitioning of Africa, Asia and Latin American Countries at the Berlin Conference of 1884 and 1885. The entrenched colonial economy was characteristically developed to achieve the aforementioned objectives and to ensure the emergence of a dependent capitalist economy characterized by primary production exchanged at unequal terms at the municipalities.

Globalized privatization

As discussed earlier, the dearth of fiscal resources faced by developing countries, Nigeria inclusive, negative external imbalances and the huge external debt profile were some of the factors accounting for government divestiture from public enterprises. The preponderance of neo-liberalism as an economic doctrine necessitated developing countries to seek for structural adjustment facilities from International Monetary Fund (IMF) and World Bank. At the core of their conditionalities is the implementation of economic liberalization measures inclusive of which is the privatization and commercialization of state owned enterprises. This conditionality can only be sufficiently understood in the context of the new globalization process and emphasis given to the New World Economic Order that advocated for enhanced participation by all nations developing and developed at the centre of the thrust behind privatization advocacy.

Globalization which simply is a process of intensified and broadened interdependence among nations involves processes central of which are; the integration of economic decision making such as consumption, investment and saving across countries. It is a process of creating a global market place in which increasingly all nations are forced to participate through the interconnection of sovereign nations via trade; creating structures that support and facilitate dependence and interconnection and creation of a global market place (Kwanashie, 1998).

Ownership of state enterprises cut across the developing world with varied objectives and goals motivating their emergence depending on individual country's peculiarities. However, central to all is the paucity of financial resources by the private sector in the early stages of political independence, in the dearth of managerial and entrepreneurial capacity of the private sector, the need to institutionalize a coherent import substitution industrial base and the strategic sector argument in order to assert and protect national interest. Neo-liberal economics assert that, the Notion of a comatose/infant private sector today does not hold sway in view of the massive income earned by local business in the last forty years due to massive improvement (increase in the gross domestic product (GDP) comfortably reflected in improved per capita income even though disproportionately distributed. The local entrepreneurs have learnt over the years new and improved skills, techniques and strategies for ownership and management of business to effectively own and manage economic activities controlled by the state.

In addition, they argued against the perpetual inefficiency associated with the operations of state enterprises compared with their counterparts in the private sector. This is measured in terms of managerial, technical, financial and scale efficiencies.

Their third argument borders on the need to utilize scarce fiscal resources more efficiently by freeing them from the clutches of bureaucratic red tape in state enterprises. Massive doses of investment, grants and subsidies to the state enterprises in most countries neither satisfy the concept of allocative efficiency nor is in consonance, with realizing an optimum net return on investment (profit). The private sector is more abreast with investing in activities that satisfy allocative efficiency and based on their superior technical and managerial skills ensure an optimum net return on investment/profitability as argued by the neo-liberal advocates.

Furthermore, the neo liberal advocates view political interference in the management of state enterprises and nepotism as one of the key malaise that render comatose these hitherto ambitious and promising state investments. New owners through privatization are free from political interference and nepotism, hence factor combinations, resources allocation and investment decisions are swiftly done with less formalization and stronger efficiency. This argument under scores the fragility of investment decision in certain areas that are adjudged private sector relevant. Increased private sector involvement does not mean that the government has no role to play. The state still had to define policies and strategies for the sector and finance socially valuable projects that are too risky to attract private investment at viable rates of return (Estache 2001). Privatization is an alternative source of attracting foreign direct investment needed to generate output, growth, employment and income in the developing countries. In the context of a freer capital and resource flows advocated by the paradigm of globalization, technically competent and financially capable core investors have emerged to take over ownership, management and control of the newly privatized enterprises. The scope and scale of efficiency is lifted up and economics of scale reaped. Across various sectors: telecommunications, power and steel, transportation, hotel and hospitality, banking and insurance, petroleum and gas, mining and mineral extraction, the story is the same of a giant, globally operating transnational corporation emerging as a core investor in the privatized arrangement. In some instances, it becomes a technical adviser to a supposedly indigenous firm that successfully emerges as a core investor. In other arrangements, it is granted a franchise to operate on a lease or a build, operate and transfer arrangement.

Conglomerates such as British Telecomm, Alcatel of France, French Telecomm, Nokia of Sweden, Erickson of Finland, Conoco Oil of the United States, Hyatt Regency of the United States, Asea Brown Boberi of Sweden, to mention just a few have utilized fully the instrumentality of their regional trading arrangements characterized by doses of government support and preference to accumulate comparatively larger capital and resource base that facilitated their competitive ability to bid and pay for such concessions and stock offered in developing countries privatization programme. It must be emphasized that regional trading blocks such as the European Union (EU) and the North American Free Agreement (NAFTA) were instrumental in the emergence of financially stronger and managerially competent trans-national corporation alliances in the quest for free capital and resource mobility. Much as the new owners in the privatized concessions promised the privatizing nation states, employment, income, fiscal linkages, output and technological transfer; these issues cannot be explained outside the context of the driving motive behind the resource flows to the "emerging markets" or developing countries. Inputs and materials are relatively cheaper providing a basis for reaping economics of scale and profitability. There exists an already captive market that can be exploited to operate profitably, but above all the consolidation of the dependency network initiated by international capital in the colonial period. Indeed several economists have argued that the newly privatized enterprises only result in private monopolies or oligopolistic market arrangements dominated by the transactional corporations.

Furthermore, the essence of privatization is to make resource savings through reduced budgetary allocation in the form of grants, subventions and subsidies to the state owned enterprises by diverting same to the provision of other social services characterized by a much stronger form of market failure and negative externalities. This is aimed at alleviating the fiscal burden of the state imposed by public utilities coupled with the desire to involve the private sector in financing the expansion of these sectors (Chisari, Estache and Romero 1995). The role of the state as a better provider of such services that market cannot produce and sale due to price indeterminacy is enhanced and consolidated through the privatization scheme. The nagging question that is often asked is; does the potential savings through reduced fiscal allocation to the state enterprises can readily and effectively be diverted to the provision of social overhead capital capable of generating maximum social benefits equivalent to the resources so saved, it is often hotly debated due to the fiscal in accountability of the Nigerian State which is quite contrary to the principle of efficiency that it is vigorously working to enforce through private control and ownership of hitherto inefficient, resources draining, bureaucratically politicized and loss making state enterprises that are seen as drain on tax payers resources. Indeed, privatization in Nigeria is linked to the globalization phenomenon based on the preference and advocacy for core investors as major shareholders in the emerging private enterprises. Many a times, prospective Nigerian shareholders either lack the technical expertise or capital or both that are needed to qualify as a core investor.

This usually necessitated emergence of alliances and technical partnership to either provide the capital or technical expertise or both. The inherent danger in this arrangement is that it usually resulted in the new technical partner dominating technical, financial and management decisions that serve more the interest of the parent company at the expense of the Nigerian partners and the ordinary Nigerian at large.

Summary, recommendations and conclusions

Having assessed in not too greater a detail, the mechanism of neo-liberal paradigm as a dominant ideology and economic policy in a world that is increasingly globalized. This increased phenomenon of globalization is manifested through trade and capital flows factors mobility, improved information and telecommunication technology and the convergence of hitherto heterogeneous cultures and values that care little for the economic, political and social aspirations of developing countries. Yet the developing countries even though weaker in institutional capacity to exploit fully the advantages associated with the globalization trend and mitigate the potential problems that could arise from such economic political and cultural diversion, there is the need to reassess their strategies in the implementation of policies especially those that surrender their economic pillars to a globally oriented and financially exploitative trans-national corporation.

Suffice it to say that privatization as a global phenomenon is seemingly an acceptable trend, popular participation through carefully conceived and implemented strategies for mass economic empowerment is meaningful if only the quest for democratization is to be relevant in the newly emerging societies where voters are no longer subjects but citizens.

References

Abdullahi, Y.Z. (2001) "An Assessment of the Impact of Privatization Policy on Public Enterprises in Nigeria: An Empirical Study of the Cement Company of Northern Nigeria (CCNN)." Paper Presented at the Annual. National Conference on Social Sciences Administration in the 21st Century organized by Faculty of Social Sciences & Administration in the Usman Danfodio University, Sokoto January 22-24, 2001.

Central Bank of Nigeria (1988) "Trends in Globalization of the World Economy and Implications for Nigeria," Proceedings of a seminar organized for executive staff of CBN, August 31 – September 1, 1998, Kaduna.

Chrisari, O., A. Estache and C. Romero (1999) "Winners and Losers from the Privatization and Regulation of Utilities: Lessons from a General Equilibrium Model of Argentina," *The World Bank Research Observer*, 13(2) pp. 357 –378.

Darma, N. A. (2000) "Public Goods, Externalities and Nigeria's Privatization Programme: Issues and Challenges," *Journal of Economics & Allied Fields* 1 (1) pp. 104–114.

Darma, N. A. (2001) "The Instrumentality of Market Mechanism and Nigeria's Privatization Programme in a Democratic Era. Analysis of Impact," Paper presented at a seminar organized by the Nigerian Economics Students Association, Uniabuja Chapter, September 12 – 14, 2001.

Darma, N. A. (2001) "Market Forces and Crisis of Development, the Paradox of Privatization," Paper Presented at the Annual National Conference of Social Sciences and Administration in the 21st Century organized by Faculty of Social Sciences & Administration in the Usman Danfodio University, Sokoto January 22–24, 2001.

Dalc, T. and M. Bale. (1998) "Public Sector Reform in New Zealand and its Relevance to Developing Countries," *The World Bank Research Observer*, 13(1) pp. 103 – 122.

Dyck, A. (2001) "Privatization and Corporate Governance Principles. Evidence and Future Challenges," *World Bank Research Observer* 16(1) pp. 59 – 84.

Estache, A. (2001) "Privatization and Regulation of Transport Infrastructure in 1990," *World Bank Economic Review* 16(1) pp. 85 – 108.

Guaseh, J. L. and W.R. (2000) "Costs and Benefits of Resulation in Developing Countries," *World Bank Research Observer* 14(1) pp. 137 – 157.

Husain, I. and R. Faruqee (1996) *Adjustment in Africa: Lessons from Country Case Studies*, World Bank Publishers.

Magaji, MA. (2001) "Public Sector Inefficiency: The Claim of Privatization Contesting Issue," Paper Presented at the Annual. National Conference on Social Sciences Administration in the 21st Century organized by Faculty of Social sciences & Administration in the Usman Danfodio University, Sokoto, January 22–21, 2001.

Ramamurti, R. and R. Vernon (1995) *Privatization and Control of State Owned Enterprises*, Economic Development Institute of the World Bank.

Shapiro, E. (1978) *Macro Economics Analysis*, Harcourt Brace Jovanovich, New York.

Sheidu, A.D. (2001) "Globalization and Human Development in Nigeria: Linkages. Implications and Challenges," Paper Presented at the Annual National Conference on Social Science Administration in the 21st Century organized by Faculty of Social Sciences & Administration in the Usman Danfodio University, Sokoto January 22 – 24, 2001.

Shirley, M. and J. Nellis (1993) *Public Enterprises Reform. The Lessons of Experience*, Economic Development Institute, World Bank.

World Bank (1995) *Adjustment in Africa: Reforms, Results and the Road Ahead*, Oxford University Press pp. 99–130.

World Bank (1996) *From Plan to Market: World Development Report*, Oxford University Press.

Williamson, G.J. (1997) "Globalization and Inequality Past and Present," *World Bank Research Observer* 12(2) pp. 117 – 135.

Yahaya, S. (1993) "State Versus Market: The Privatization Programme of the Nigerian State," in Olukoshi O. A. (ed.) *The Politics of Structural Adjustment in Nigeria*, Heinemann Educational Books, Ibadan, pp. 16–31.

10

Globalization and ecological problems in Nigeria

– S.A.J. Obansa

Abstract

Nigeria lost grip over agricultural produce as the major source of foreign exchange to oil products when the latter became more prominent and exploited at commercial level starting from the mid 1970s. However, environmental experts say, both agricultural and oil exploitation have potentially contributed to environmental degradation over the years. The chapter attempts to focus, in the face of globalized world on the issue of good environmental management in an effort to address soil erosion, deforestation, water contamination, air pollution, and other forms of ecological problems on environment. It has been recognized that immediate government intervention would help to alleviate social tension, conflicts between communities and oil producing firms, and stem measures to eradicate poverty and promote economic and social *improvement especially in areas with serious ecological problems.*

Background

The economy of the nation largely depends on natural resources based activities. Before the discovery of oil at commercial quantity in 1975 agriculture was basically the major source of income of the country coming from various agricultural products such as yams, cocoa, rubber, palm oil, maize potatoes, tomatoes timber, kola nuts, rice and all sorts of fruits and vegetables located in rain forest belt of the country while crops like potatoes, dry season tomatoes, onions, carrots, upland rice, cattle, groundnuts, cotton, soya-beams, sorghum, maize, millet, wheat, etc. from Savannah zone. For instance, in 1970-71 agriculture accounted for about 36 per cent of the country's gross domestic product (GDP) while mining and quarrying contributed 33 per cent. In 1974-75, agriculture's contribution fell to about 23 per cent while that of mining and quarrying rose to 46 per cent. In 1979, agriculture's contribution fell to less than 70 per cent and has remained at low point (Chiesho, 1983). He stressed further that food import has been on increase from the amount of 46.9 million spent in 1962 to ₦95.1 million in 1972 and over ₦1 billion in 1992. Whichever way one looks at it, agricultural production has suffered a setback in the Nigerian economy. However from this zonal classification of both food and cash crop it is apparent that Nigeria is blessed with variety of food crops and the economic activities of the people were therefore basically agricultural on which they derived their livelihood.

Similarly Nigeria is rich in mineral deposits. These include both liquid and solid minerals such as petroleum products, coal, marble, clay, limestone, tin, lead, galena, tantalite, uranium gold, bitumen, salt and assorted precious stones and gypsum. These are found at different locations of the country and they have contributed immensely and are still contributing to the economic progress of the country (see Appendix A). The discovery of petroleum production in mid 1975 in large commercial quantity in Nigeria by the multinational oil companies in collaboration with the country over turned the role of agriculture as the prime income earner for the country. Suffice to say oil production has been playing this leading role as the major source of foreign exchange for the country. This means that while the activities in oil exploration and exploitation intensify that of agriculture slow down even though it is still expected to provide the source of food supply and raw materials for domestic agro-based industries. From the foregoing therefore it is quite clear that the source of ecological problems can be traced to the combined activities in both agricultural and mineral production in Nigeria. However, the problems vary from one region to another depending on the nature of economic activities being operated in that area:

(a) Incidence of overgrazing especially in the Northern and middle belt of the country thereby exposing the topsoil to serious natural disaster.

(b) The ecological character of wetlands is modified by changes in water regimes which result from agriculture, industrial hydropower development and over exploitation of timber, fish and wildlife resources of the area, especially in the forest zone.

(c) The activities of oil exploration and exploitation in the South Eastern part and partly Western area of the country have unleashed untold consequences on the environment and the people around the area which has led to serious environmental degradation and eventual loss.

These, no doubt, have resulted in serious ecological problems, which have attracted the attention of the government in an effort to reduce the attendant consequences on the environment. The question that will readily come to mind is, can Nigeria resolve these problems alone without the help of international community given the magnitude of the situation? Perhaps, the answer may be found in the ideals of globalization, which has reduced the entire world into close contact in terms of technological and economic advancement taking place within it.

This chapter therefore, examines the habits of living things in Nigeria as they relate to their immediate environment and as they fit into the globalized economy. The remaining sections of this chapter discuss some issues on environmental management in Nigeria, resource control and its controversies, community rivalries and oil installation vandalism, significant environmental protection policies in Nigeria and some specific programmes designed to resolve ecological problems in Nigeria.

What is meant by ecology?

Ecology is described as the study of relationship of plants and animals to their physical and biological environment. The physical environment includes light and heat or solar radiation, moisture, wind, oxygen, carbon dioxide, nutrients in soil, water and atmosphere while the biological environment talks about the organisms of the same kind as well as other plants and animals.

This implies that ecology is the study of the economy of nature in the sense that it seeks to explain how organisms attempt to adapt to their environment through natural selection (Darwin, 1859).

The functional units of ecosystem represent the population of organisms through which energy and nutrients move, interacting in various ways in order to produce desired effects which are of benefit to themselves and man within the immediate environment. In a community of animals and plants known as habitat, they have specific roles played by each of them called niches. For instance some insects which live in certain zones discharge their role in pollinating flowers which eventually culminates in fruits production for human consumption as well as for other animals and plants. Similarly other organisms have their roles to play to ensure that they are not only economically useful to themselves but also to other organism in the community.

If the mission of globalization is to ensure a unity of purpose amongst the people of the world, it means that ecosystem becomes a world concept and as a result joint efforts should used in ensuring environmental protection particularly in some parts where there appear signs of environmental degradation. The issue of environmental protection is not only the immediate concern of the people that live within the environment but also the concern of those that remotely live outside it who are endowed with resources required to maintain it.

However, if this fails to happen, it means that globalization appears to be exploitative against the less endowed segment of the globalized society.

Nigeria is divided into four major vegetational zones. The southern zone which is of mangrove and rain forest type comes under serious threat as a result of active extraction of mineral oil, while in the middle belt which is mainly dominated by savannah suffers similar soil degradation due to overgrazing of animals and solid minerals extraction and while in the northern part is constantly threatened by desert encroachment. All these forms of interdependence and interaction with environment appear to have contributed in no small measure in environmental degradation and attendant ecological problems for which the country is saddled with the responsibility of providing the solutions. This therefore calls for prudent environmental management on the part of the country, to ensure that decent environment is maintained through sound environmental policy.

Environmental management in Nigeria

Natural resources are said to be wasting assets in the sense that they reduce in quantity and content as vigorous exploitation is increasingly taking place. This implies that environmental degradation begins to set in and as such there is need for concerted effort to support and manage the environment in order to maintain the quality of life of people that live around the area.

The ability of strengthening and sustaining economic growth in Nigeria therefore depends on the expressed desire of the country to evolve a sound environmental management policy in dealing with environmental degradation. As Reed (1992) documented in the case of Thailand, it is quite possible to have a situation where the structural reforms reduce environmental pollution per unit of output but where the increase in output is so high then the net result is environmental deterioration. This is not the type of policy that is being contemplated here.

This calls for prudent management of resources that we have and which must be channelled to support the emergence of depleting environment. This should be accompanied with environmental legislation, regulation and policies or co-ordinating the implementation of existing instruments (World Bank: 1996). The report in question identifies the respective roles of the government, the private sector, local communities, NGOs and other donors in ensuring the virile and sustainable environmental management. Since environmental issues are important and to some extent contribute in shaping the prospect of economic development of a nation it should not be treated with levity as if it is an ad hoc affair. The World Bank report on environmental management points out the following management objectives to be integrated into the overall planning and development process: These include institutional reform, participatory approaches through the process of consultation among different public sector agencies at the central, district, and local level and NGOs, prioritization of issues, legal and policy reform and donor co-ordination which most African countries especially rely on for assistance for public investment and capacity building.

Resource control and its controversies

Resource control appears to be a political and orchestrated campaign emanating from oil producing states from where a large proportion of exportable crude oil, which contributes significantly to the foreign exchange of the country, is derived. The issue of resource control has attracted significant contributions either in favour or against it. As Sagay (2001) rightly remarked, the deluge of views being expressed on the matter has succeeded in generating awareness among the people about what they contribute to national development as a result of oil exploration and exploitation taking place in their area.

The resource control arguments could be summarized mainly on economic ground. The oil producing areas felt they have been neglected in terms of economic development for a long time. According to them, the areas lack good roads, dependable electricity, portable water and other social amenities while other areas whose contribution to the national coffers is meagre enjoy all the comfort of life that the country can offer to them. In this respect, they cited places like Abuja, Lagos and some big cities in Northern states of the country where life is said to be rosy with milk and honey in those places. On their own part they are only contented with frequent oil spillage polluting the environment and a threat to life every now and then, soil degradation, mass killing of fishes and other animals as a result of oil exploitation, which goes on in the area on daily basis.

Resource control as defined by Sagay (2001) is the right of the states and communities most directly concerned (that is the producing states and communities) to have a direct and decisive role in the exploration for, the exploitation and disposal of, including sales of the 'harvested' resources. He went further to say that people who live with the devastating consequences of greedy, cheap, crude, reckless and irresponsible exploitation practices and procedures should control the mode and management of commercial production in order to ensure an environmentally friendly production process, elimination of pollution, protection of the lands, forest, rivers, and atmosphere. There is no doubt, this view point as it may sound convincing requires constitutional arrangement that will be reflected in the Federal structure of governance where a clear definition of political responsibility and relation between the Federal Government and the state would be made.

Community rivalries and oil installation vandalism

In recent times, there were series of ethnic crises amongst the tribal communities of the Niger-delta states of the country. They argued that their areas have been neglected in terms of provision of social amenities, educational development by the federal government. Coupled with these is the hostile attitude of the oil prospecting companies to assist in the development of projects that would improve the socio-economic conditions of the people in oil producing areas.

The militia youths of the areas occasionally take laws into their hands to stop the prospecting activities of the oil companies. In fact, such conflicts between the indigenes and oil workers usually resulted in high death tolls. In addition, oil pipelines and other petroleum installations were vandalized. All these actions by the youths of the area are measures aimed at showing their displeasure against the oil companies and the federal government.

Adenuga (1999) clearly stated that despite the effects or impacts of oil exploration and production in the Niger Delta on the ecology and environment of the area, the oil companies operating in the country have paid little or no attention. He therefore offered a way out in form of studies on this aspect, which would pay greater dividend in ameliorating the conflict situation or foster close relationships between the communities and oil companies operating in the area. In this respect, the first bold attempt in promulgating a law towards environmental protection was in 1968 when Oil in Navigable Water Decree was enacted. A year after, the Petroleum Decree No. 51, in 1969 came into force. The decree specified that oil corporations should:

> adopt all practical precaution...to prevent the pollution of inland waters, rivers, water courses... by oil, and other fluids or substance which might contaminate the waters, banks and should take prompt steps to control it.

Adenuga (1999) however, observed two fundamental loopholes in this decree.

Firstly, the decree did not take into consideration the onshore operations where the oil spillage is more likely to affect agricultural lands. Secondly, it was equally silent on the nature of compensation to be made to victims of such disasters. This implies that, the onus now falls on the oil companies to determine what compensation to pay in the event of any pollution. The oil company would rather choose to contaminate the water if the cost of preventing it is higher than what they hope to pay as compensation. However, the experience of the dumping of toxic waste in Koko, a seaport in Delta State prompted the government to enact Decree 42 in 1988, which dealt on the Harmful Waste (Special Criminal Provision, etc.). This decree among other thing prohibited the purchase, sale, importation, transit, transportation and storage of harmful waste in the country. A life imprisonment for those who contravene its provision was prescribed.

Globalization as a received concept is meant to bring countries with different economic and social background together for mutual benefits in economic and technological development. The spate of technological development in developed countries has no doubt enhanced the advances made in area of environmental protection of those places, which perhaps have resulted in indiscriminate dumping of harmful waste in other places. In spite of globalization tendency being drummed into our ears, Nigeria and indeed other developing countries have not experienced the dividends of this new development. The limited access to the use of technological innovations due to high cost has negatively affected the lives of individuals in this part of the world.

However to keep to the minimum standard of environmental protection, the country has taken a bold step in enacting a decree (No.58 of 1988) in which a body known as the Federal Environmental Protection Agency (FEPA) was established with the following terms of reference:

(i)   The responsibility for protection and development of the environment in general, and environmental technology including initiation of policy in relation to environmental research and technology.

(ii) Advising the Federal Government on national environmental policies and priorities and/on scientific and technological activities affecting the environment.

(iii) Preparing periodic master plans for the development of environmental science and technology and advising the Federal Government on the financial requirement for the implementation of such plans.

(iv) Carrying out such other activities as is necessary or expedient for the full discharge of the function of the agency under the decree FEPA Decree 1988.

However, in spite of all these notable steps taken towards a better environmental friendly condition, environmental degradation gets worse day by the day as remarked by the UNDP report (1998). This is manifest in air and water pollution, urban decay, and unhealthy environment, which aggravate human poverty while soil erosion, flaring of gas and toxic waste, exacerbate income poverty. In fact, UNDP (1988) observed that in such circumstances, sustainable human development is a realistic option because it promotes both poverty eradication and good environmental practices.

Programmes designed to address ecological problems in Nigeria

Apart from environmental policy option, some physical measures have been put in place aimed at poverty alleviation of the victims of the environmental disaster. Such measures include Ecological Disaster Funds, Oil Mineral Production Area Development Commission (OMPADEC), budgetary allocation to oil producing states and local governments, and to say the least the community relation programmes of the oil-producing firms.

However, the general objectives of these funds have been subjected to serious abuses, ranging from poor management and embezzlement at both executive and local levels to non-allocation of funds at all. For example,

OMPADEC was bedevilled with poor financial management and embezzlement to the extent that its activities further degraded the environment and unleashed untold hardship on the beneficiaries of such funds. The government was not left in doubt as to what to do with it other than to scrap it and replace it with a new body to perform the same purpose. In this respect the National Assembly had passed a bill entitled Niger Delta Development Commission (NDDC) in no distant future. It is hoped that NDDC will not be one of OMPADEC's, which served as conduit pipe for siphoning funds into individual pockets.

The aim of the Commission is to manage two per cent allocation of funds to oil producing areas for poverty alleviation of the people whose living conditions have been neglected over the years while

In the words of Idisi (1998), the general ecology is degraded and damaged as spills persist; fishing waters and associated livelihood pursuits are lost thereby leading to increased economic burden as well as fall in rural income.

Plan of action

The government should avail itself of the globalized world to reverse the process of environmental degradation. It is our belief that if the Niger-Delta Development Commission takes off with good environmental management as priority in its operation it would resolve some of the contending problems associated with ecological issues in Nigeria especially inter-communal wars and the hostile attitude of the host communities towards oil exporters would be averted.

In most cases, good environmental programmes have been killed in the process of implementation through embezzlement and other forms of corruption on the part of government officials. The immediate impact is poor delivery of the programmes, which translate into poor living conditions of the supposed beneficiaries.

Summary and conclusion

Nigeria has been depending on natural resources for her source of livelihood as a nation. The exploration and exploitation of these resources have left serious ecological problems to tackle within her limited resources. It was observed that what the country requires to solve the ecological problems is the sound environmental management. The government, in addressing the consequences of environmental degradation FEPA decree, has enacted many decrees including. The Niger Delta crises and the issue of resource control can be traced to the living conditions and expression of unjust treatment in terms of poor allocation of funds for economic development of oil producing area. Because of this, many programmes of action, which include establishment of a body known as NDDC, which is expected to look into the aspect of economic development of the area, have been put in place.

It is hoped that if these measures are vigorously pursued with the attention it deserves, it would help to put to rest socio-political tensions which occasionally griped the area.

References

Adenuga, A. O. (1999) "Petroleum Industry and Protection: Nigeria Experience," *Bullion,* Volume 23 No.4; Central Bank of Nigeria Publication, Lagos.

Ama, E.O.A (1992) "Keynote Address: Nigeria's Environmental Balance Sheets" in Alna E.O.A and N.O. Adedipe (eds.) *Environmental Consciousness for Nigeria National Development* (monograph 3) Lagos: Federal Environmental Protection Agency.

Chiesho, P. (1983) "Agriculture – An alternative to Oil," *Business Times,* Monday November 14 1983, p. 15.

Darwin, Charles (1859) *The Correspondence of Charles Darwin Vol.7: 1858-1859 by Charles Darwin,* University of Cambridge Press, 1991.

FACU, (1994) "Environmental Impact Assessment of the National Fadama Development Project (Southern States-Nigeria)," Report prepared for Federal Agricultural Co-ordinating Unit (FACU) Abuja.

Federal Office of Statistics, Lagos (1970) *Federal Republic of Nigeria: Annual Abstract of Statistics,* FOS, Lagos pp.73.

Idisi, P.O. (1998) "Problems and Programmes for Poverty Alleviation in Crude Oil Conditioned Environments of Nigeria," A Paper presented at Conference on Poverty Alleviation in Nigeria held at the Department of Economics, Edo State University Ekpoma, 13th – 17th July.

Imam, A. (2000) "Women's NGOs criticise the introduction of so-called Religious Law which abuse women's rights," in Vicky MS., Molemodile Ltd, Uwani Enugu.

Reed, David, (ed.) (1992) *Structural Adjustment and the Environment,* Boulder, Colorado: WWF-International West View Press.

Sagay I. (2001) "Federalism, the Constitution and Resource Control: My Response," *The Guardian,* Monday, August 13th 2001, Lagos.

World Bank, (1996) "Towards Environmentally Sustainable Development in Sub-Sahara Africa: A World Bank Agenda Manufactured In the United States of America."

UNDP, (1998) *Nigeria Human Development Report,* United Nations Development Programmes, Lagos, Nigeria.

Appendix A: Distribution of the major mineral resources of Nigeria

S/NO	MINERAL	LOCATION/KNOWN DEPOSIT	RESERVES (MT)
1	Kaolin	Kankara (Katsina State); Onobode J. Ushabi, Barmago, Miroko (Ogun State), Jos, Kop (Plateau State); Maiduguri, Biu (Borno State); Unwunzi (Delta State); Garkida (Taraba/Adamawa); Won, Igbotako (Ondo State)	3 billion
2	Barytes	Azare (Bauchi); Awe (Benue); Akin Hall (Plateau); Wukari (Adainawa)	500,000
3	Bentonite	Azare (Bauchi); M./Balewa (Adamawa)	
4	Gold	Ilesha (Osun State); Edo State, Niger State and Sokoto State	2 million
5	Limestone	Nkalagu, Odomoke (Enugu State); Nfamosing, Odukpani (Cross River State); Ewekoro/Shagamu (Ogun State); Igumale, Ogbolokuta-Tandev (Benue State); Ashaka, Kanawa (Bauchi State); Kalambaina (Sokoto State); Omno-Obom, Olafia (Abia State)	
6	Marble	Jakura Ubo, Ajaokuta (Kogi State); Kankara (Katsina State); Toro Muro Hill (Plateau State)	1.5 billion
7	Dolomite	ECT Oyo, Elebu, Osara, Kogi State, Ukpila, Igara, Ikposhi-Edo State	
8	Talc	Ilesha – Osun State Sanlu – Kogi State Kagara – Niger State	40 million
9	Gemstone	In large commercial quantities in some state-Kaduna, Benue. Kano, Plateau, Oyo and Onun.	
10	Columbia	J_{05} Area	500,000
	Tantalite	Jos Area	20,000
12	Phosphate	Sokoto Baro-Ogun State, Anambra, limo, Edo Bularabe, Abakire-Yobe State	N/A
13		Diantomite	10 million
14	Gypsum	Potiskum, Damboa-Yobe/Borno States, Wurnor, Gada, Kukanmje-Sokoto Shelleng-Adamawa, Anambra, estimates Ofun, Imo, Edo Benue and Bauchi State.	141.4 million

11

Globalization and the environment

– Said Mashi Abubakar

Introduction

The term 'environment' conventionally defined as the collection of living and nonliving elements constituting an area, that exist in some delicate and intricately linked relationships. In this regard, the elements to which reference is given here include racks, vegetation, climate, human beings, man-made features and soils. Because of the intricate and delicate nature of the relationships that do exist between such elements, a reference is correctly being made to the environment as a typical working system. As a system, it is consequently being expected that the environment will have a capability to undergo some adjustments once if the working of its system is tempered with. Such adjustments may have both negative and positive consequences on the various environmental elements depending upon the way in which the working is tempered with. Because the consequences may be adverse, the concern for long in most societies has been on the impact of manipulations (especially by human activities) of the working of the environmental system.

Over the last ten years especially with the collapse of communism during the early 1990s, deliberate efforts have been made by nations of the world to move closer to each other to facilitate more nation-to-nation interactions. As the result, the hitherto isolated nation states such as the communist countries of Libya and Iran, and the "Island" communist American nation of Cuba started reaching out to other nations, and are being reached to by so many other nations, including even their hitherto arch enemies such as the USA. The dissolution of bipolar world arrangement in favour of the unipolar one has therefore tremendously facilitated close interactions between and among nation states of the world[3]. With these enhanced interactions, the urge in recent times has been on the need for the world to now be looked at as more of a global community than anything else. As a result, the world is now seen as a "global village" in which nations have greater access to each other. This globalization phenomenon has in some recent years attracted substantial academic discourse, especially as regards what it is, what it is not, what it can, what it can't, why it must be, why it must not be, what are its real and potential benefits, among others.

It is not the aim of this chapter to carry out an evaluation of such a discourse. Rather, the aim here is to appraise the phenomenon within the context of the impact it will have on the global environment. The remaining parts of this chapter are divided into five parts. In the first one the ideology of globalization is thoroughly discussed while in the second one its salient features are discussed. In the third one, a model was developed and discussed to show the environmental influence of globalization. In the final part, the main conclusions that could be reached at from the discussions of the chapter are presented.

The confused ideology of globalization

Globalization can be regarded as a very confined ideology. This is mainly because while in principle it is considered as a process of bringing the nations of the world together, in practice it is pursued as a process of fusing the global economy into a micro-unit (the so-called village), which will facilitate its effective manipulation, by those over whose hand the global economy circulates. While simple economic logic provides that productive processes progress provided land, labour, capital and entrepreneurship are available, at a global scale it is now apparent that foreign capital investment to which a nation gets access to once such a nation is "globalizes", is all that is needed for such processes to commence. Not surprising for instance, when Nigeria turned democratic again, we were left in no doubt by the "global" community that effective productive processes in the country can only be guaranteed if we create an enabling environment for inflow of direct foreign capital investment, the fact that we have land, labour, capital base and entrepreneur not withstanding.

Globalization is therefore being deliberately confused with expansion of global capitalism, such that any nation that fails to embrace the expansion is being considered as an opponent of globalization. Today globalization is seen more in terms of transfer of ownership of enterprises from public to globally organized private hands, many of whom are either controlled by located at, or have link with the developed nations of the world (the centre) from where capitalism spreads. In most African countries, such a transfer (popularly called privatization) is now being religiously pursued. Because the periphery (the so-called less developed) nations have for long been "globalized" politically and socio-culturally, the new globalization campaign is seen as a vehicle for final, complete economic globalization in the world.

Salient features of globalization

The tempo at which the present globalization campaign is being prosecuted is analogous to that of a hurricane blowing over an isolated island, inhabited by people and structures existing in a hopeless situation. Under such a situation, the hurricane is typically offered no resistance. In the world today, the rate at which globalization is being embraced far outweigh that at which its promoters are promoting it. There is consequently no nation of the world that is not being affected by the glowing wind of globalization. The main features of the ongoing globalization campaign include:

(i)   Enhanced networking and connectivity between nations of the world through advances in information technology. This has made it possible for cultures and civilizations to spread, products to be marketed, and business opportunities, including investment, to be opened-up.

(ii) Aggressive promotion of backward and forward capital linkage is between the centre and periphery, of foreign capital in the name of investment and economic development.

(iii) Promotion of limitless private ownership of virtually everything. This has been making it possible for those with financial might (the mode of acquiring the wealth notwithstanding) to acquire substantial share of hitherto state-own enterprises in especially the periphery. This campaign is being prosecuted under the guise of privatization.

(iv) Unhindered repatriation of gains, sometimes wholly, from points of investment. This has been making it possible for profits to limitlessly be exported out of, especially, the periphery to particularly the centre.

(v)   Increase in international trading with hitherto semi-closed markets now being open-up for outside goods and service. This has particularly made it possible for products from especially the periphery to now be reaching markets in places such as Eastern Europe and the former Soviet Union. Likewise, most African markets are now flooded with finished products that make locally produced ones to be witnessing reduced patronage.

In many respects therefore, globalization is a means by which western capitalism is spreading out but rather than through conquests and colonialism, but now by dialogue, trade treaties, multilateral and bilateral pacts, and mental colonization. In fact even the major promoters of globalization, such as the World Bank, now see the major gains of globalization as being "rising share of international trader in world output and in the extraordinary rise in capital mobility including foreign direct investment.

Environmental influence of globalization: towards an explanatory model

It is clear from the salient of globalization as presented above that it operates within an environmental context. As such it is no doubt expected to have some influences on the environment, whether negative or positive, slight or heavy.

Figure 1 has been developed here as a model for explaining the nature of such influences. On the basis of this model it is apparent that some linkages do exist between a number of processes and activities associated with globalization campaign and environment. In the first instance, campaign for globalization has been influencing (and is being influenced by) enhanced connectivity between nations of the world, and desire for improved productivity. The two are being facilitated by the tremendous progress that is daily being made in information and related technology which make communication and production processes to be greatly improved. Because of these, nations of the world are now developing policies that are aimed at making such nations to become part of the globalization process. With such policies in place, those nations are now witnessing some improvements in inflow of foreign capital, expertise and other inputs necessary for productive processes. The nations are also having an improved access to information on resources that are potentially available for such processes. Likewise, trade between and among nations is now being enhanced greatly. These have no doubt been improving economic activities in the affected nations. They have equally been facilitating greater influx of foreign goods into those nations (i.e., increased imports). In Nigeria for instance, foreign goods including things such as biscuits, toothpaste and canned drinks can now be found almost everywhere, even in remotest settlements.

Increased imports and intensification of economic activities in "globalized" nations of the world are associated with five things that have some potentially serious effects on the environment. First, demands for raw materials to sustain the improving economic activities are now on the increase. According to simple law of energy conservation, whenever resources are extracted, wastes must be generated, since energy cannot be destroyed. Likewise, the demands could facilitate aggressive exploitation of resources, which inevitably can create problems such as resource degradation, and biodiversity losses. Second, as more emphasis is placed on economic development as a nation globalizes, an imbalance is created between desire to develop and the need to effectively manage the environment. In particular, more emphasis is typically placed on the urge to develop with environmental management relegated to a second fiddle, and sometimes largely ignored. In the Niger Delta of Nigeria for instance, emphasis is typically given more on oil extraction than protecting the environment from abuse. Such an imbalance, as is practically being experienced in Nigeria, usually promote environment-induced social conflicts. The third dimension has to do with the indirect effect which economic activities (such as industrial manufacture) do have on the environment. Since globalization promotes increased tempo in economic activities it is to be expected that environmental problems that are associated with such activities, especially air, water and soil pollution, would become important. The fourth has to do with the effect of increased consumption of finished products on wastes generation. As consumption behaviour changes with more finished products being imported, wastes generation is expected to increase. This aggravates wastes-induced pollution problem and makes effective management of wastes to become difficult.

The fourth dimension of influences of globalization on the environment is the environmental crises that may develop on the long run, whose magnitude may be variable depending upon the tempo of the activities generated by the globalization campaign.

It is apparent that modern development trend as being preached through globalization is more of myth than reality. It is in fact most likely to promote underdevelopment of the so-called developing nations at the expense of continuous development of the already developed nations. Reason for this is simple: Development in developing nations is tied closely to the environment and since globalization is most likely to promote its abuse and devastation, then globalization is to best be seen as a vehicle for consolidating underdevelopment.

Summary, conclusion and recommendations

Globalization has remained one of the most successful campaigns ever embarked upon by the developed nations of the world in their spirited efforts towards bringing the whole world under complete capitalist control. The campaign is being pursued not by force, but by treaties and dialogue with virtually every nation now aspiring to be part of the global village. The implication of this now is that most borders are now collapsing under free trade, international capital is flowing freely across must borders, and many nations are aggressively mobilizing resources at their disposal in order to be part of this fast moving train.

Unfortunately, on the long-run, the environment (both built and natural) is at the receiving end, as environmental crises of varying dimensions are apparently being generated. However because the emphasis in most nations now is on what dividends are derivable (especially in economic terms) from the current wave of globalization, not much emphasis is being placed on the enormous negative consequences which globalization potentially has on environment. There is thus the need for empirical research to be conducted in nations of the world on the practical consequences of globalization on the environment.

Fig. 1: Linkages between globalization and environmental crises at a national scale

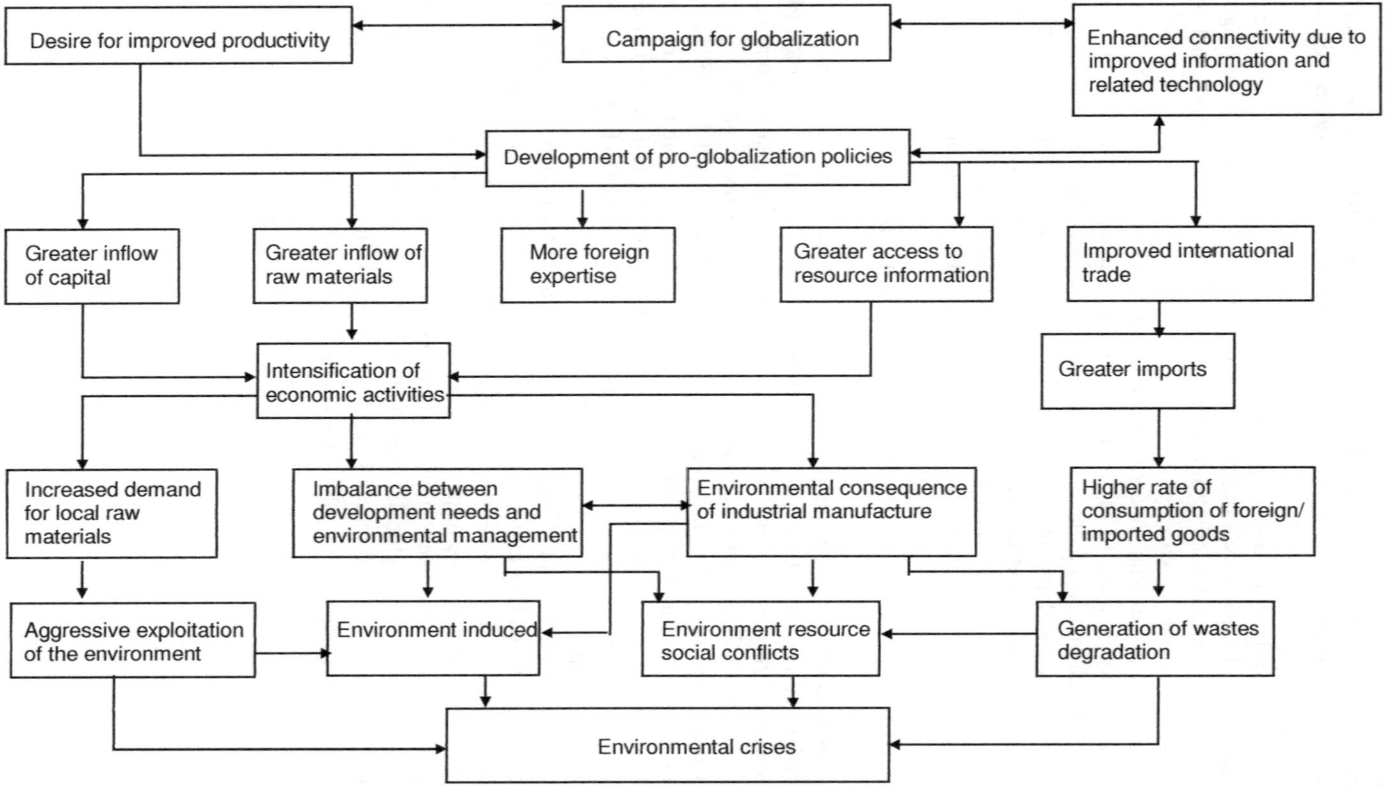

References

Bell, S. (1995) *Sharing the Wealth: Privatization Through Broad-Based Ownership Strategies*, The World Bank, Washington DC.

Berthoud, G. (1990) "Modernity and Development," *The European Journal of Development Research* 2: 1-13.

Crocker, D.A. (1991) "Towards Development Ethics," *World Development* 19: 5-16.

Economic Intelligence Unit (1994) *The EW Global Privatisation Manual: A Practical Guide to the Process and Practitioners*, Cambridge University Press, Cambridge.

Haque, I. U. (1995) *Trade, Technology and International Competitiveness*, Economic Development Institute, The World Bank, Washington D.C.

Human Rights Watch (1999) *The Price of Oil: Corporate Responsibilities and Human Rights Abuse in the Niger Delta, Nigeria*, Human Rights Watch, London.

Isma'il, M. (1995) *Political Economy of the Development Agenda in the 1990s and Beyond*, United Nations University, Tokyo.

Mannion, A. M. (1993) *Environmental Issues for the 1990s*, Longman, London

Rist, G. (1990) "Development as part of the modern myth: The Western Socio-Cultural Dimension of Development," *The European Journal of Development Research* 2(1): 20-29.

Rist, G. (1999) *Growth Inequality and Globalization,* Cambridge University Press, Cambridge.

Sader, F. (1995) "Privatizing Public Enterprise and foreign investment in developing countries (1983-1993)," *Foreign Investment Advisor Service*, Occasional paper 5, International Finance Corporation/World Bank.

Schmidheing, S. (1992) *Changing Course: A Global Perspective on Development and the Environment with the Business Council for Sustainable Development*, Massachusetts Press, Massachusetts.

Simail, M. (1995) *The Evolving New Global Environment for the Development Process*, United Nations University, Tokyo.

World Commission of Environment and Development (1987) *Our Common Future*, Oxford University Press, Oxford.

12

The new globalization era and digitalization debate: an economist's perspective

– Godwin Chukwudum Nwaobi

Introduction

In almost all of the thirty reports it has published since "The Limits of Growth (1972)", the authors (Club of Rome) do not only describe and analyze the complex problems facing the world (world problematic), they are essentially keen to offer projections which point to constructive paths into the future.

Hence, there can be no doubt that 'globalization' has become one of the trendiest words in fashion as new millennium emerges. It is pertinent to note that this phase does not reflect an inevitable natural phenomenon but rather, is indicative of a process, which has to be structured on any number of differing levels. Thus, our main concerns will be to deal with on the global level, two long-term goals of equal importance: environmental sustainability and socio-economic equality. These goals often stand in contradiction to each other but strategically seen, they are nevertheless interdependent.

Globalization, then, is a process that has to be structured quickly and in a positive way. If this is to be systematically achieved, the population of the world will have to assume a high degree of responsibility for a common future. Humanity's future will only be secured if our intercourse with nature becomes more respectful, sparing, and sustainable. This will require not only all of our efforts to make use of technical advances to increase efficiency, but will also demand that we develop new sustainable life-styles which, at least, in part will require some material renunciation. It is against this background that the rest of this chapter is divided into five sections. Section two looks at the concept of globalization. The inequality and non-sustainability problems are respectively the focus of sections three and four. The digitalization process as a global solution is presented in section five while section six concludes the chapter.

Globalization

Indeed, globalization is not new, but the present era has distinctive features. Shrinking space, shrinking time and disappearing borders are linking people's lives more intensely, more immediately than ever before. That is, people everywhere are becoming connected – affected by events in far corners of the world. Here, we have new markets (foreign exchange and capital markets linked globally, operating twenty-four hours a day, with dealings at a distance in real time); new tools (Internet links, cellular phones, media networks); and new actors (the world trade organization with authority over national governments, the multinational corporations with more economic power than many states, the global networks of non-governmental organizations and other groups that transcend national boundaries); and new rules (multilateral agreements on trade, services and intellectual property, backed by strong enforcement mechanisms and more binding for national governments, reducing the scope for national policy). The challenge of globalization in the new century is not to stop the expansion of global markets but to find the rules and institutions for stronger governance – local, national, regional and global – to preserve the advantages of global markets and competitions; and also to provide enough space for human, community and environmental resources to ensure that globalization works for people (UNDP, 1999).

In this sense, globalization is shaping a new era of interaction among nations, economies and people. It is increasing the contacts between, people across national boundaries – in economy, in technology, in culture and in governance. But it is also fragmenting production processes, labour markets, political entities and societies. So, while globalization has positive, innovative, dynamic aspects - it also has negative, disruptive, marginalizing aspects. Today's interactions between nations and people are deeper than ever as shown by global trends and links in Table 1 below. Driving this global integration are policy shifts to promote economic efficiency through the liberalization and deregulation of national markets and the retreat of the state from many economic activities, including the restructuring of the welfare state.

Driving integration even faster are the recent innovations in information and communications technology. But global integration is still very limited given that the flow of labour is restricted across regions. However, the world today has more opportunities for people than hundred years ago. Child death rates have fallen by half and a child born today can expect to live a decade longer than a child born then. In developing countries, the combined primary and secondary enrolment ratio has more than doubled - and the proportion of children in primary school has risen and forms less than half to more than three-quarters. Also, adult literacy rates have risen and more states are now independent with more than seventy percent of the world's people living under fairly pluralist democratic regimes. But these trends make great unevenness in the advances and in the new setbacks. Despite the tremendous progress in the 20th century, the world today faces huge backlogs of deprivation and inequality that leave huge disparities within counties and regions.

Global governance therefore is the framework of rules, institutions and practices that set limits on the behaviour of individuals, organizations and companies; and hence the intergovernmental policy-making in today's global economy is in the hands of the major industrial powers and international institutions they control (the World Bank, International Monetary Fund, and the Bank for International Settlements).

Their rule making may create a secure environment for open markets, but there are no countervailing rules to protect human rights and promote human development. More so, ad-hoc and self-selected policy groups have emerged in the past decade to make *de facto* global economic policy, outside the United Nations or any other formal system with democratic processes and participation. Some of these groupings include G-7, G-22, G-15, and G-10. All these groups play a key part in international economic policy-making, yet only the G-22 has any consultation with developing countries, and then only with a select few. And yet, one big development in opening opportunities for people to participate in global governance has been the growing strength and influence of NGOs. They have been effective advocates for human development, maintaining pressure on national governments, international agencies and corporations to live up to commitments.

Inequalities (insecurities)

Indeed, globalization has its winners and its losers. With the expansion of trade and foreign investment, developing countries have seen the gaps among themselves widen. Meanwhile, in many countries, unemployment has soared to levels not seen since 1930s, and income inequality to levels not recorded since the last century. This picture is clearer by looking at the parameters of global inequalities/insecurities in Table 3. In fact, uneven globalization will bring not only integration but also fragmentation – dividing communities, nations and regions into those that are integrated and those that are excluded. Again, Social tensions and conflicts are ignited when there are extremes of inequality between the marginal and the powerful. Research on complex humanitarian emergencies (see UNDP, 1999) have revealed that "horizontal inequalities" between groups - whether ethnic, religions or social groups are the major cause of the current wave of civil conflicts

Inequalities (insecurities) matter not only in incomes but also in political participation (in parliaments, cabinet, armies and local governments), in economic assets (in land, human capital and communal resources), in social conditions (in education, housing and employment). Again in most countries, dislocations from economic and corporate restructuring and dismantled social protection have meant heavy job losses and worsening employment conditions. Jobs and incomes have become more precarious. Again, the pressures of global competition have led countries and employers to adopt more flexible labour policies, and work arrangements with no long-term commitment between employer and employee are on the rise.

Table 1: Global trade links

	Merchandise exports (Million of dollars)		Export of commercial services (Million of dollars)		Merchandise Imports (Million of dollars)	
	1983	1998	1983	1997	1983	1998
World	1,757,216	5,414,844	356,892	1,326,312	1,755,569	5,358,567
Low income	88,785	334,896	10,869	51,538	102,719	295,254
Excluding China and India	-	-	5,457	18,068	-	-
Middle income	410,520	953,662	57,320	230,847	381,036	1,018,458
Lower middle income	-	239,691	27,570	101,056	205,214	370,345
Upper middle income	225,563	622,990	30,088	130,233	184,578	647,211
Low and middle income	493,984	1,288,084	68,072	282,785	482,412	1,313,145
East Asia and Pacific	97,271	537,234	12,292	105,518	101,854	411,054
Europe and Central Asia	-	249,450	-	77,725	-	309,720
Latin America and Caribbean	99,355	270,876	14,268	44,471	74,429	337,406
Middle East and North Africa	118,705	103,782	14,926	30,412	123,259	113,156
South Asia	14,868	50,743	4,457	12,396	25,032	67,304
Sub-Saharan Africa	49,231	84,706	6,603	13,026	51,878	86,534
High Income	1,271,830	4,124,433	288,345	1,043,005	1,278,838	4,040,845
World	377,843	1,307,618	-	-	192,662	400,394
Low income	21,228	85,092	14,819	88,685	5,732	59,509
Excluding China and India	17,369	44,337	4,840	19,551	2,083	11,922
Middle income	87,836	247,297	28,091	210,049	18,697	103,780
Lower middle income	35,868	103,897	-	-	-	-
Upper middle income	51,234	143,661	-	-	-	
Low and middle income	107,707	332,063	42,910	298,734	24,429	163,295
East Asia and Pacific	17,773	128,602	18,720	104,257	11,135	64,284
Europe and Central Asia	-	59,655	7,695	49,875	1,097	22,314
Latin America and Caribbean	21,329	63,390	12,411	118,918	8,188	61,573
Middle East and North Africa	38,488	36,039	622	7,899	2,711	5,240
South Asia	5,329	17,494	2,174	11,110	464	4,662
Sub-Saharan Africa	14,347	25,133	1,288	6,674	834	5,222
High income	271,116	977,279	-	-	168,233	237,099

Sources: World Development Report (1999); Human Development Report (1999)

Indeed, globalization opens many opportunities for crime, and is rapidly becoming global out-pacing international co-operation to fight it. Today, there are many drug users, threatening neighbourhoods around the world. Illegal trafficking in weapons is a growing business - destabilizing societies and governments, arming conflicts in some continents. Another thriving industry is the illegal trafficking in women and girls for sexual exploitation, a form of slavery and an inconceivable violation of human rights.

Table 2: Parameters of global inequality and insecurity

		Real GDP per capita (Ppp$)	Human develop ment index value	Gender- related develop ment index (GDI)	Human poverty index HPI (%)	GNP per capita (US$)
		1997	*1997*	*1997*	*1997*	*1997*
1	All developing countries	3,240	0.637	0.630	27.7	1,314
2	Least developed countries	992	0.430	0.415	44.9	260
3	Sub-Saharan Africa	1,534	0.463	0.454	40.6	522
4	Arab State	4,094	0.626	0.609	32.4	1,754
5	East Asia	3,601	0.712	0.709	19.0	1,330
6	East Asia (excluding China	14,300	0.849	0.743	-	11,811
7	South-East Asia and the Pacific	3,697	0.695	0.692	25.0	1,556
8	South Asia (excluding India)	1,803	0.544	0.525	36.6	452
9	South Asia	2,147	0.542	0.524	38.6	670
10	Latin America and the Caribbean	6,868	0.756	0.749	14.5	3,953
11	Eastern Europe and the CIS	4,243	0.754	0.752	-	2,249
12	Industrial countries	23,741	0.919	0.915	13.5	27,174
13	World	6,332	0.706	0.700	-	5,257

In this case, women lose not only their freedom, but also their dignity and often their health if they return to their homes, their families and communities often reject them. At the heart of all, this is the growing power and influence of organized crime syndicates. The sheer concentration of their power and money criminalizes business, politics and government. All have operations extending beyond national borders, and they are now developing strategic alliances linked in a global network, reaping the benefits of globalization. Again, civil conflicts have been flaring for decades. But what's new today is the complex interaction of interests, the blurred line between conflicts and business. Defence is becoming privatized, and international private military firms are proliferating. Accountable only to those who pay, such businesses are hard to regulate and so far domestic and international laws seeking to limit mercenary operations have been ineffective.

Unsustainability

At the end of the twentieth century, environmental problems are a matter of both national and global concerns. Many of them create spill-overs that impose heavy costs not only on those close to the source of the problem but also on society as a whole and on future generations. Individual countries have strong economic and social reasons for aggressively protecting their environments by creating incentives to reduce and manage such spill-overs. Yet, an important subset of environmental problems is global in scope. Many counties have contributed to these problems, and no individual country can effectively address them by acting alone. These are the problems of the "global commons", which will place all countries at risk if no collective action is taken. There are many such issues, including desertification, persistent organic pollutants, the fate of Antarctica, and the environmental health of the high seas and the seabed.

However, biodiversity destruction and climate change are two pressing problems in the global environmental agenda. Table 4 reports the current state of these problems. Indeed, economic activity is the driving force of climate change and biodiversity destruction. Both originate in current pattern of consumption and resource use. As shown in the Table 4, the economic activity of industrial nations which house less than 20 per cent of the world population originates greater percent of global emissions of carbon dioxide that could potentially change the global climate. The destruction of forest ecosystems that accompanies industrialization is believed to be the main source of global biodiversity loss. Thus, fossil fuels and forest destruction are at the root of the global environmental problems. Industrial society depends on fossil fuels, and industrialization has led to most of the destruction of the world's forests in contemporary society. From this perspective, without changing industrial countries' patterns of consumption, and resource use, there would be no solution to the world's global environmental problems.

Yet, the contribution of developing countries is more ambiguous and complex. Many developing countries have embarked on, and aspire to their own process of industrialization. If, however, they were to replicate the pattern of resource use of industrial countries, fifty years from now they could become the major source of global environmental damage: this could spell disaster. Again, the developing countries are the source of most exports of natural resources used in the world. Here, industrial countries' extensive use of resources is associated with resource – intensive patterns of economic growth in many developing countries, patterns that have prevailed since the end of colonial rule fifty years ago. The situation has been summarized as the developing countries over-exploitation of resources, which are exported and over-consumed in the industrial countries.

As evidence about the potential seriousness of the effects of climate change has mounted, attention has focused on the likely costs of different policies to slow or halt the change. Numerous studies have investigated the possibilities of reducing the emissions of green house gasses, the cause of global warming, with most attention being focused on CO_2. The most important greenhouse gas and various economic models have been developed to examine the likely cost of reducing such emissions (see Nwaobi, 1999c). These models have mostly concentrated on man-made emissions of CO_2, which arise almost entirely from the burning of fossil fuels, so that energy-sector detail has been of importance. There have already been several surveys of these model results (Howeller *et al*, 1991; Boero *et al.*, 1991 and Cline, 1992).

But each of these surveys has been confronted with the problem of trying to compare like with like, the model results generally being for a variety of different time periods, key baseline assumptions, reduction scenarios and so on. Even with a standardization of assumptions on growth, population and resources, the ball emission paths vary greatly across the models. This is already a point of concern since the costs of achieving any target level for emissions such as the stabilization at 1990 levels, depend critically on the nature of the baseline (what "distance" does one need to cut). In such "target" cases, it is not only the absolute tons of carbons that will vary across models but also the proportionate cut. The CO_2, emission paths in the ball scenario are shown in Table 4.2. Here, there are some differences in the starting point for energy–related CO_2 emissions in 1990, ranging from 5.8 billion tons of carbon (GREEN, WW, ERM) to 6.0 billion tons (CRTM and MR). This initial difference of 3 per cent is not trivial, but it is also not surprising given that 1990 data are estimates based on data on energy consumption in earlier years and the application of "carbon emission coefficients" for different categories of fuel. In fact, the difference in 1990 level of emissions look relatively small when compared with the divergences in CO_2 emissions that open up, even in the short-term (for the world).

In Table 5 it is clear that world emissions grow rather more rapidly over the short to medium term in GREEN and IEA than in the other models. ERM shows the slowest emission growth. Up to 2020, emissions in GREEN are growing by up to ½ per cent per annum faster than in ERM, despite the assumption of the same autonomous energy efficiency improvement of 1 per cent per annum. Hence a gap of over 1½ billion tons of carbon opens up by 2020 between the top and bottom of the range of models, the 10.8 billion tons or GREEN and the 8.2 billion tons of ERM. But looking beyond 2020, where it is possible to make direct comparisons of time paths for only CRTM, ERM, MR and GREEN (up to 2050), the divergent emissions parts for only CRTM, ERM, MR and GREEN (up to 2050), the divergent emission part for the earlier period open up much further.

Table 3: Some other indicators of global inequality and insecurity

Debt Service Ratio % Exports	Dependency ratio %		Female economic activity rate			Refugees		Suicides (100,000)		Prison 100,000 per		Gender empower ment measure
			% Rate	1985 = 100	% of Male rate	By country of asylum ('000)	By country of origin ('000)	Male	Female			
1985	1997	1997	2015	1997	1997	1997	1997	1997	1990-95	1990-95	1994	1994
28.7	18.4	62.5	50.7	39.3	111.3	68.0	7,669.6	-	-	-	238.8	0.3798
20.5	12.4	84.8	70.8	41.1	99.7	76.5	2,749.1	2,704.5	-	-	204.4	0.2814
25.2	13.7	91.4	77.6	37.8	97.7	73.9	2,770.0	2,005.4	-	-	-	-
-	-	74.3	57.4	19.2	123.7	38.6	763.3	-	-	-	-	-
18.5	8.6	47.5	40.6	55.1	114.2	86.6	292.7	119.8	-	-	-	-
27.8	8.6	41.2	41.1	41.2	126.1	69.7	-	-	-	-	-	-
30.5	14.7	60.0	45.8	41.7	118.6	74.1	-	-	-	-	-	-
15.8	19.9	68.1	49.8	29.1	99.4	51.7	3,559.2	-	-	-	-	-
10.9	20.5	76.5	55.8	29.5	114.2	55.9	3,336.1	300.6	-	-	-	-
38.1	35.6	61.5	50.2	28.8	140.0	51.3	83.2	-	-	-	-	-
-	9.8	51.2	44.7	45.6	97.3	82.4	835.0	1,069.4	51.9	10.5	225.7	0.5767
-	-	49.7	52.7	41.9	119.4	72.6	2,753.3	-	19.5	5.7	233.4	0.4513
-	-	59.6	50.6	40.2	111.3	69.8	11,975.5	-	-	-	-	-

Sources: World Development Report (1999); Human Development Report (1999)

Of course, what may look to be relatively small differences in annual growth rates of CO_2 emissions compound over a century into significant differences in terms of levels. The average growth rate of emissions over the whole of the period 1990-2100 is 1.3 per cent in ERM, 1.6 per cent in CRTM and 1.7 per cent in MR. But the spread between the lowest and highest emissions in 2100 22 '/2 billion tons of carbon in ERM and 39 '/2 billion tons in MR is quite startling. WW have a point estimate for 2100 of 65 ½ billion tons but this seems to reflect both an extremely pessimistic assessment of energy efficiency improvements and the lack of substitution possibilities imposed by the two-fuel structure of the model. Thus, the importance of the autonomous energy efficiency parameter (AEEI) in contributing to the large differences in emissions has been revealed by some sensitivity test.

Table 4: Global environmental problems

| | Annual Deforestation 1990–1995 | | National Protected Areas (1996) | | Carbon dioxide emissions | | | | CO₂ emissions | | SO₂ emissions per capita (kg) | GDP per unit of energy used | |
| | | | | | Million metric tons | | Per capita metric ton | | % capita fossil fuel | Share of the world total % | | | |
	Square KM	Average annual % change	('000) Sq Km	% of total land area	1980	1996	1980	1996	1996	1996	1995	1980	1996
World	101,724	0.3	8,542.7	6.6	13,640.7	22,653.0	3.4	4.0	62	93.8	41.78	3.1	3.2
Low income	49,332	0.7	2,439.4	5.9	2,126.1	5,051.8	0.9	1.5	72	0.4	-	-	-
Excluding China and India	-	-	-	-	-	302.0	690.9	0.0	0.6	-	-	-	0.8
Middle income	64,086	0.3	2,809.9	4.8	2,804.5	6,871.5	3.0	4.8	69	36.0	41.25	2.4	1.7
Lower income	21,162	0.2	1,563.6	4.3	1,150.1	4,194.9	2.0	4.8	72	-	-	1.7	1.0
Upper middle income	42,924	0.5	1,246.3	5.7	1,654.4	2,676.6	4.0	4.7	61	-	-	2.8	2.6
Low and middle income	113,418	0.4	5,249.3	5.3	4,930.6	11,923.3	1.0	2.5	69	36.4	41.25	1.4	1.3
East Asia and Pacific	29,956	0.8	1,102.2	6.9	1,958.5	4,717.5	1.0	2.7	81	-	-	-	-
Europe and Central Asia	-5,798	-0.1	768.0	3.2	886.9	3,412.7	-	7.4	68	-	-	-	0.8
Latin America and Caribbean	57,766	0.6	1,456.3	7.3	848.5	1,209.1	2.0	2.5	32	-	-	3.5	3.2

| | Annual Deforestation 1990–1995 | | National Protected Areas (1996) | | Carbon dioxide emissions | | | | CO₂ emissions | | SO₂ emissions per capita (kg) | GDP per unit of energy used | |
| | Square KM | Average annual % change | ('000) Sq Km | % of total land area | Million metric tons | | Per capita metric ton | | % capita fossil fuel | Share of the world total % | | | |
					1980	1996	1980	1996	1996	1996	1995	1980	1996
Middle East and North Africa	800	0.9	242.0	2.2	493.6	986.9	3.0	3.9	93	-	-	2.2	1.6
South Asia	1,316	0.2	213.0	4.5	392.4	1,125.1	0.0	0.9	79	-	-	0.7	0.9
Sub-Saharan Africa	29,378	0.7	1,467.8	6.2	350.7	472.1	0.0	0.8	79	-	-	-	-
High income	-11,694	-0.2	3,293.4	10.8	8,710.2	10,730.6	12.3	12.3	58	43.8	42.31	4.1	5.0

**Table 5: Worldwide (BAU) Business as Usual CO_2 emissions
(billion tons of carbon)**

	CRTM	ERM (1)	ERM (2)	GREEN(1)	GREEN(2)	IEA**	MR (1)	MR (2)	WW
1990	6.003	5.767	5.767	5.815	5.815	5.919	6.003	6.003	(Average of 1990 to 2100 is 25.2
2000	6.931	-	-	7.071	7.418	7.316	6.970	6.748	
2005	-	6.709	7.856	7.704	8.250	7.932	-	-	
2010	8.031	-	-	8.705	9.452	-	8,153	7.581	
2020	9.327	8.180	10.505	10.806	11.938	-	9.520	8.681	
2050	11.337	11.838	17.606	18.998	21.769	-	14.992	11.356	
2080	23.519	18.099	32.185	-	-	-	26.945	18.701	
2100	35.863	22.578*	41.594*	-	-	-	39.636	26.039	65.5

Notes: *   2095

       **   The LEA model projections in this table have been adjusted to exclude non-fossil solid fuels, bunkers, non-energy use of fossil fuels and petrochemical feed stocks. These categories included in the standard LEA model output have not been excluded from the tables in the appendix or from the result reported in the LEA paper and add around 900 million tons to the 1990 global figures of carbon emissions.

      ***   In the three cases (ERM, MR, GREEN) where two emission paths are indicated, the first column denotes the standard model and the second column shows the sensitivity to a different assumption on the autonomous energy efficiency improvement (AEEI). ERM (I), GREEN (1) and MR (2) have an AEEI of 1 per cent per annum while ERM (2), GREEN (2) and MR (1) have an AEEI of *A* percent per annum.

    ****CRTM is the carbon Rights Tmde Model (See Rutherford, 1992); ERM is the Edmonds–Reilly Model (See Bams *et al*, 1992); GREEN is the OECD Model (See Oliveira Matins *et al*, 1992); LEA is the International Energy Agency Model (See Vouyoukas, 1992); MR is the Mane-Richels Global 2100 Model (See Mane, 1992) and WW is the Whalley-Wigle Model (See Whalley and Wigle, 1992)

In an alternative BAU scenario, using ERM but reducing AEEI from 1 percent per annum to ½ percent in all regions, world emissions rise from the previous 22-A billion tons to around 42 billion tons by the end of the next century, much in line with the MR results.

A similar exercise with MR, this time increasing its AEEI to 1 per cent per annum in all regions, leads to emissions in 2100 of 26 billion tons, much closer to the standard ERM result of 22 ½ billion tons. On the other hand, imposing a lower AEEI of ½ percent in GREEN takes the 2050 emission to a higher level (21.8 billion tons compared with 19 billion tons using the standard model with a 1 percent AEEI).

It is therefore very evident that the world faces a major challenge: to find practical paths for sustainable development. This means finding ways to reorient consumption patterns and use of natural resources in ways that improve the equality of human life, while living within the carrying capacity of supporting ecosystems. It requires building economic systems where basic needs are satisfied across the world, while protecting resources and ecosystems so as not to deprive the people of the future from satisfying their needs.. It also requires building a future in which humans live in harmony with nature and we are far from this goal. Indeed, in many ways, the world economy is moving in the opposite direction and the task is daunting.

Digitalization

Digital technology describes not only the digitalization of communication but also an entire plethora of new processes and instruments. The microelectronic revolution at the beginning of the 1980s, as well as modern satellite technology and fibre optic cables played a decisive role in all this. All of these things have produced a wide range of new products: mobile telephones, e-books, pagers, players, notebooks, recorders, and so on. These discoveries are consequently leading to what might be called the knowledge revolution. Here, an important input is knowledge rather than information. This is basically the difference between the computer industry, which is based on information technology, and other sectors such as telecommunication, biotechnology and nano technology, which involve knowledge. In other words, knowledge is the content while information is the medium. Thus, the content is driving change, facilitated by the medium.

A distinct possibility therefore, is that in the mid 21st Century, a new society will develop, a society that is centred in human creativity and diversity, and which uses information technology rather than fossil fuels to power economic growth. This vision is a human-centred society, which is deeply innovative in terms of knowledge and at the same time very conservative in the use of natural resources. The patterns of consumption and resources use may not be as voracious as those in the industrial society and may be better distributed across each society and across the globe. This knowledge society may achieve economic progress that is harmonious with the nature. This vision is distant and only a possibility at present. Without developing the right institutions and incentives, this possibility may never come to pass, and a historical opportunity may be lost. Table 5.1 shows the current structure of information and communication technologies in the world. To produce new knowledge, economic incentives are necessary. This could involve restricting the use of the knowledge by others, so the creator can benefit. Patents on new discoveries work in this fashion: by restricting the use of knowledge and this creates a problem. Any restriction in the sharing of knowledge is inefficient, because knowledge could be shared at no cost and by doing so, it can better others. So, restrictions on the use of knowledge are inefficient after knowledge is created. However, without some restrictions there may be no incentive to create new knowledge and this could be called the paradox of knowledge. Here, the solution to the paradox could be a new system of property rights that can deal simultaneously with the need to share the use of knowledge for efficiency, while at the same time preserving private incentives for production. These systems ensure and encourage widespread use of knowledge, while at the same time offering incentives to private individuals, the knowledge creators to produce new knowledge.

Specially, we propose substituting patents by a system of compulsory negotiable licenses, which are traded in the market competitive along with all other goods in the economy. In this new scheme, the right to knowledge is unrestricted; however, users must pay the creator each time they use their knowledge. Since the license is traded in competitive markets, they ensure that the creators of knowledge are compensated for their labour in a way that reflects the demand for their products and therefore their usefulness for society.

In this sense, it is pertinent to note that the newest technologies (computers, genetic engineering and nanotech) differ from the technology that preceded them in a fundamental way. They are self-accelerating; that is the products of their own processes enable them to develop evermore rapidly. New computer chips are immediately put to use in developing the next generation of more powerful ones, which is the inexorable acceleration expressed as Moore's law. The same dynamic drives biotech and nanotech – even more so because all these technologies tend to accelerate one another. Most recently, computers are rapidly mapping the DNA in human genome and now DNA is being explored as a medium for computation. When nanobots are finally perfected, you can be sure that one of the first things they will do is make new and better nanobots. Technologies with this property of perpetual self-accelerated development (auto catalysis) create conditions that are unstable, unpredictable and unreliable. And since these particular autocatalytic technologies drive whole sectors of society, there is a risk that civilization itself may become unstable, unpredictable and unreliable. In fact, the economic destiny and prosperity of entire nations may rest on one question: can silicon based computer technology sustains Moore's law beyond 2020?

The secret behind Moore's law is that chipmakers double every eighteen months or so, the number of transistors can be crammed into a silicon water, the size of a fingernail. They do this by etching microscopic grooves into crystalline silicon with beams of ultraviolet radiation. A typical wire in a Pentium chip is now 1/500 the width of a human hair. the insulating layer is only 25 atoms thick. But the laws of physics suggest that this doubling cannot be sustained forever. Eventually, transistors will become so tiny that their silicon components will approach the size of molecules. At these incredibly tiny distances, the bizarre rules of quantum mechanics take over permitting electrons to jump from one place to another without passing through the space between. Hence electrons will spurt across atom-size wires and insulators, causing fatal short circuits. More so, transistor components are fast approaching the dreaded point - one limit – when the width of transistor components reaches 0.1 microns and their insulating layers are only a few atoms thick. Recently, some scientists have therefore sounded an alarm warning that Moore's law could collapse and that there are currently no known solutions to these problems.

However, the search for a successor to silicon has become a kind of crusade; it is the Holy Grail of computation. Among physicists, the race to create the Silicon Valley for the next century has already begun and some of the theoretical options are explored. The optical computer replaces electricity with laser light beams. Unlike wires, light beams can pass through one another, making possible three-dimensional microprocessors. Thus, the optical counterpart of a desktop computer would be the size of a car. Again, one of the most indigenous ideas being pursued is to compute using DNA, treating the double-standard molecules as a kind of biological computer language (except that instead of encoding 0s and is in binary, it uses the four nucleic acids, represented by A, T, C, G). This approach holds much promise for crunching big numbers. Hence large banks and institutions may one day use it. However, DNA computer is an unwieldy contraption, consisting of a jungle of tubes of organic liquid, and is unlikely to replace a laptop in the near future. Other exotic designs include the molecular computer and the quantum dot computer (which replace the silicon transistor with a single molecule and a single electron respectively). But these approaches face formidable technical problems, such as mass-producing atomic wires and insulators; and viable prototypes yet exist. The darkest horse to emerge in this race is the quantum computer, sometimes dubbed the ultimate computer. The idea is to direct a laser or radio beam on a carefully arranged collection of atomic nuclei, each of which is spinning like a top. As the beam bounces off the atoms it flips the spines of some of them and analyzing how the spins have been flipped can perform complex computations.

Clearly, none of these designs are ready for prime time. Most are still on the drawing board and even those with working prototypes are too crude to rival the convenience and efficiency of silicon. There may be a silver lining to all this. If Moore's law somehow continues unabated, then by some estimates, our computers by 2050 will be calculating well beyond 500 trillion bytes per seconds (per secs), at which point, they will be considerably smarter than we are. In other words, there is still a room for creativity and designers are still going to have to think. Computers will become a lot more transparent and you won't recognize you are using one. People with little education are going to be able to participate and the digital division is going to disappear.

For the future of the Internet, most access will probably be via high-speed, low-power radio links. Most hand held, fixed and mobile appliances will be Internet enabled. This trend is already discernible in the form of internet-enabled mobile telephones and personal digital assistants (PDA) equipped with radio links, a PDA can serve as an appliance-control remote, a digital wallet, a cell phone, an identity badge, an e-mail station, a digital book, a paper and perhaps even a digital camera perhaps. This could be called Wireless Internet Digital Gadget for Electronic Transactions, (WIDGET). Again, so many appliances, vehicles and buildings will be on-line by 2020 that it seems likely there will be more things on the Internet than people. Internet-enabled cars and aeroplanes are coming on-line, and smart houses are being built everyday. Eventually, programmable devices will become so cheap that we will embed them in the cardboard boxes and these passive "computers" will be activated as the pass sensors and will be able to both emit and absorb information. Such innovations will facilitate increasingly automatic manufacturing, inventory control, shipping and distribution. The advent of programmable, nanoscale machines will extend the Internet to things such as the size of molecules that can be injected under the skin, leading to Internet– enabled people. Such devices, together with Internet-enabled sensors embedded in clothing, will avoid a hospital stay for medical patients who would otherwise be there only for observation. The Internet will also undergo substantial alteration as optical technologies allow the transmission of trillions of bits per seconds on each strand of the Internet's fibre–optic backbone network. The core of the network will remain optical and the edges will use a mix of access technologies, ranging from radio and infrared to optical fibre and the old twisted-pair copper telephone lines. Here, more and more of the world's information will be accessible instantly and from virtually anywhere. In an emergency, our health records will be available for remote medical consultation with specialists and perhaps even remote surgery. More and more devices will have access to the global positioning system (GPS) increasing the value of geographically indexed databases. Using GPS with speech understanding software, we will be able to get directions from our WIDGETS. However, in the face of the internet – wide virus attacks, is the realization that we will depend in larger and larger measure on the network's functioning reliably - making this system of millions of networks sufficiently robust and resilient is a challenge for the present generation of Internet engineers (with an optimistic view of the future).

Without the means to electronically evaluate data, future scientific research remains unthinkable, therefore scientists has recently announced the "source codes of *homo sapiens*" – an approximate reading of the chemical sequence of the human genome. This genome is all the deoxyribonucleic acid (DNA) that makes up an organism. Genes (over three billion) are apart of the complex biological process of making those proteins, which determines how an organism looks, feels or behaves. This may spell the beginning of the biotech age, plus megabucks for biotech industries. But beyond the economics are the immense benefits this new discovery holds. For instance, in the area of molecular medicine, detailed genome maps have aided researchers to discover genes associated with various diseases. In such instances, doctors can now treat the actual causes of diseases rather than mere symptoms. In addition, diagnostic tests can be more specific medical researchers may also be able to produce genome specific drugs and there is the increased likelihood of improve gene therapy. Here, microbial genomic (understanding the genomes of micro-organisms) could help in providing new energy sources (bio fuels), environmental monitoring to detect pollutants, protection from chemical and biological warfare and more efficient toxic waste clean up. In addition, understanding the human genome will enable scientists to understand the effects of exposure to things like radiation and other energy–related agents. And yet, other benefits are in DNA forensics, agriculture, livestock breeding, bio-processing and the production of "made to order" babies. It is however the later, more than anything else, that has been a subject of raging controversy and thus has been seen as tinkering with the Almighty God (Our Divine). Indeed, future developments along this line should be discouraged.

Conclusion

Indeed national action is essential to capture global opportunities in trade, capital flow and migration and to protect people against the uncertainties and vulnerabilities of globalization. But the success of national action hinges on how effectively countries can negotiate at the global level. Thus reinventing global governance is not an option but an imperative for the twenty-first century. Global competition and market efficiency are the big objectives of current efforts to restructure global economic governance. The latter needs to incorporate human development priorities for people in all parts of the world (for poverty reduction, equity, sustainability and human development). Here, the institutions of global governance have leaned hard on national governments to adopt their preferred systems of social protection – marginal for the International Monetary Fund, social safety nets for the World Bank and a broader and more pragmatic range of social policy options and mechanisms for other United Nation agencies.

But a broader, more coherent set of international principles is required -as some governments are beginning to recognize. Such agreements, carefully defined can raise living standards and protect the environment, without setting back employment or discouraging foreign investment. Collective regional action can ensure that the decisions are based on the needs of people in the countries concerned. In other words, with the new challenges of globalization, and the need to ensure stronger action on old problems and new, the time has to come to rethink the global architecture. Some of the key element of the proposed international architecture are a stronger and more coherent UN system, with greater commitment from all countries; a global central bank; a world investment trust with re-distributive functions and transfer mechanism; a world environment agency; a revised world trade organization; an international criminal court and a broader United Nations. These new and stronger international institutions of global governance can be global public goods. At the national level, public goods have been recognized as vital when the market is neither the incentive not the mechanism to meet a public need. With growing globalization, international public goods are now needed for similar reasons. This new perspective is much more than a change of terminology. To recognize the need for global goods is to accept the importance of actions of global governance beyond the capacity of individual countries to provide, to establish a rationale for new forms of financial support that countries need to ensure but to recognize also that without special efforts such support may not be forthcoming. These issues become matters for political advocacy and education on globalization in which all countries have a role and a stake.

Indeed, relative to today's global economy and the global challenge of sustainability, present structures and levels of global supports are minuscule. Needed is a world environment agency, possibly developed from UNEP, with much larger resources and broader functions. These include overseeing the global environment presenting reports and posing issues for review and policymaking, to broker deals and to serve as a clearing bank. One important focus of that agency would be to encourage the removal of perverse subsidies and shift the resources released to direct support of environmental protection and other measures (including employment creation) for its cleaning house functions, the agency would oversee trade in permits for green house gas emissions, along the lines explored in the clean development mechanism proposed in the climate conferences. Emission rights could be borrowed or lent, but not sold and thus keeping the market competitive and avoiding any risk that developing countries might lose long-term control over their rights. Also, the clearinghouse would be a new mechanism for mobilizing additional financial resources for developing countries, especially the poorest.

Finally, the world is rushing headlong into greater integration that is driven mostly by economic forces and guided mostly by a philosophy of market profitability and economic efficiency. People in all parts of the world need to join in the debate and to make clear their interests and concerns. The process of reinventing global governance must be broader and human development can provide framework for this exploration. This piece therefore is our own contribution.

References

Barns D. W., J.A. Edmonds & J.M. Reilly (1992) "Use of the Edmonds – Reilly Model Energy-related green house gas emissions," *OECD Economic Department Working Papers* No. 113.

Chichilnisky G. (1998a) "The knowledge revolution: Its impart on consumption patterns and resource use" in UNDP (ed.) *Background. Paper: Human Development Reports,* New York: United Nations Development Program.

Chichilnisky G. (1998b) "The Knowledge Revolution," *The Journal of International Trade and Economic Development,* 11:1, 3 9-54.

Manne A. (1992) "Global 2100: Alternative Scenario for Reducing Carbon Emissions," *OECD Economics Department Working Papers* No. 111

Nwaobi G.C. (1998) *Computing Technology and Behavioral Research: All Integrated Approach,* Cape coast: Quanterb/Njakod Press

Nwaobi G.C. (1999a) *The Economics of Year 2000 (Y2k) Millennium Bug: A Useful Guide for Computer System Users and Professionals,* Lagos: Hot-Ice Production.

Nwaobi G.C. (1999b) "Information Technology in Africa: Structure and Diffusion," A Paper presented at the Twelfth World Congress of the International Economic Association, Buenos Aires, Argentina South America (August 23-27).

Nwaobi G.C. (1999c) "Emission Policies and the Nigerian Economy: Simulations from The Dynamic Applied General Equilibrium Model," A Paper presented at the Fourth Annual African Econometric Conference, University of Witwatersand, Johannesburg; South Africa (July).

Nwaobi G.C. (2000) *The Knowledge Economics: Trends and Perspectives,* Lagos: Quanterb/Goan Communications Press

Nwaobi G.C. (2001) *Modern Econometric Modelling for Developing Economies,* Abuja: Quanterb/Goodtimes Press

Oliveira Martins J., J.M. Burniaus, J.P. Martin, & G. Nicoletti (1992) "The Costs of Reducing CO_2 Emissions: A Comparison of Carbon Tax Curves with GREEN," *OECD Economic Department Working Papers,* No. 118

Rutherford, T. (1992) "The Welfare Effects of Fossil Carbon Restrictions: Results from a Recursively Dynamic Trade Model," *OECD Economic Department Working Papers* No. 112

UNDP (1999) *Human Development Report,* New York: Oxford University Press

Vouyoukas L. (1992) "Carbon taxes CO_2 Emissions targets: Results from the IEA Model," *OECD Economics Department Working Papers* No.114

Whalley J. & R. Wigle (1992) "Results for the OECD comparative modelling exercise from the Whalley – Wigle Model," *OECD Economic Department Working Paper* No. 121.

Williamson J.G. (1997) "Globalization and Inequality: Past and Present," *World Bank Research Observer,* Vol. 12, No. 2

World Bank (1999) *World Development Report*, Oxford: Oxford University Press.

www.ingramcontent.com/pod-product-compliance
Lightning Source LLC
Chambersburg PA
CBHW021830020426
42334CB00014B/569